Do You Know the Jargon of the New Age?

- The coach of your high school swim team stresses the importance of "holistic health."
- Your company supervisor announces that all managers must attend a "self-actualization" seminar.
- Your children announce they have a new subject in school—"Values Clarification."
- While visiting a friend, she puts on some "relaxation music" she's just purchased.

Unfamiliar New Age vocabulary is popping up in familiar places—from the classroom to the board room to the living room—what's it all about?

In *From Nirvana to the New Age* briefly yet thoroughly explains all these curious terms, and many more including:

- One World Government
- Channeling
- Reincarnation
- Yin/Yang
- Biofeedback
- Networking

FROM NIRVANA TO THE NEW AGE

MARY ANN LIND

Fleming H. Revell Company
Publishers
Tarrytown, New York

Library of Congress Cataloging-in Publication Data

Lind, Mary Ann.
    From Nirvana to the new age / Mary Ann Lind.
        p.   cm.
    Includes bibliographical references.
    ISBN 0-8007-5381-X
        1. New Age movement—Controversial literature.
    2. Apologetics—20th century.   3. Cults—United States—
    Controversial literature.   4. Sects—United States—Controversial
    literature.   I. Title.
    BP605.N48L56   1991
    299'.93—dc20   90-46026
                                                                         CIP

Copyright © 1991 by Asia Life, Inc.
Published by the Fleming H. Revell Company
Old Tappan, New Jersey 07675
Printed in the United States of America

With a grateful heart, this book is
dedicated to those faithful prayer warriors who
prayed this book into existence. May our Father
bless you

Contents

Contents

IV
WHY DO PEOPLE GET INVOLVED?

V
HOW DO WE RESPOND?

Acknowledgment

Every author is deeply indebted to a variety of family, friends, and associates for their suggestions, encouragement, and assistance. For me to list the many wonderful persons who contributed significantly to the completion of this book would be at the risk of omitting someone important.

However, one person stands in a class by herself in her thoughtfulness and support. Without Beverly Haley's professional assistance and personal encouragement, I doubt this book would be a reality. Every writer should have such a friend.

From Nirvana To The New Age

I

WHAT'S IT ALL ABOUT?

1
Point of Departure

Kristen (not her real name) resembled any other college junior as she stood in the door of my office in the history department. Her sparkling brown eyes reflected the optimism and eagerness of a twenty-year-old for whom the future is a world of opportunity.

"I'm sorry I missed your class yesterday," she said.

She certainly had my attention; few students at the university where I was teaching part-time ever apologized for missing a class.

"I was up until half-past three the night before and was just too tired to come to class," she went on to explain. "I was at this professor's house and there were two men there—I think they were monks or something. They were talking about things like reincarnation, cosmic consciousness, and the universality of all mankind."

By now, I was all ears as this clean-cut young lady went on to describe the large group crammed into the professor's living room.

"The discussion went on and on. What they were talking about sounded pretty good, but I just kept thinking something was not quite right in what they were saying. Lots of kids are getting mixed up about their own beliefs."

At my invitation, Kristen came in the next day so we could talk at greater length. The topics she had heard at the evening meeting had the earmarks of a discussion involving New Age thinking. Fortunately, Kristen's Lutheran religious training told her that something about the topics discussed was not in keeping with Christian thinking.

My heart went out to the young people who were at that meeting as well as to many others across America on other campuses. What haunted me for a long time was Kristen's statement, "Lots of kids are getting mixed up." It isn't just students who are getting "mixed up" at this traditionally conservative university; many other people in all walks of life are getting mixed up as well. What they are getting mixed up in is the New Age Movement, which is rapidly taking on the earmarks of a religion in the United States, Canada, Australia and Western Europe.

From Small Town, USA, to sophisticated city circles, New Age influence can be discerned—sometimes in very subtle ways, other times in bold newspaper and magazine headlines. Corporate planners now include motivational seminars designed to restructure employees' thinking. Thousands of the curious flock to weekend retreats to hear ancient voices channeled through such instant celebrities as J. Z. Knight and Jach Pursel. Unsuspecting tourists wander into shops specializing in crystals. A full-page advertisement in a campus newspaper touts academic success through transcendental meditation. Physical-fitness buffs faithfully practice yoga deep-breathing techniques.

Are these examples unrelated, or are they the evidence of an expanding influence now evident in much of the Western world? Is the New Age based upon some grand plan, or does it simply consist of unconnected activities and modes of thinking? Is the New Age just a passing fad destined to disappear into history's trash heap?

The purpose of this book is not only to address these questions but also to answer clearly four important questions for Christians: What is the New Age? What are its roots? How can it be seen in Western culture? And, most important, what should the Christian response be?

Quite simply, Christians *must* maintain an awareness of the New Age as we see the rapid fulfillment of biblical prophecies which point to the return of the Lord Jesus Christ, the precious Bridegroom. In Matthew 24:5, Jesus said, "For many will come in my name, claiming, 'I am the Christ,' and will deceive many." As the return of Jesus Christ approaches, the New Age Movement provides a foundation, network, and vehicle for the promotion of the spirit of the antichrist as prophesied in the Bible.

For the unsuspecting, New Age vocabulary, programs, and activities offer a subtle and appealing invitation to a more relaxed, self-controlled personal existence combined with a world of peace and harmony. To the knowledgeable Christian, the New Age emerges as the antithesis of the very heart of biblical teaching. As New Age influence gains momentum, committed Christians will recognize the full meaning of Paul's exhortation in Ephesians 6:12: "For our struggle is not against flesh and blood, but against the rulers, against the authorities, against the powers of this dark world and against the spiritual forces of evil in the heavenly realms."

Perhaps the most startling aspect of the New Age Movement is that its major tenets are not "new" at all. Rather, the New Age represents part of a continuum of religious beliefs whose origins can be traced as far back as ancient Babylon A student of Hinduism, Buddhism, Taoism, and Eastern mysticism readily recognizes influences of these ancient religions upon New Age thinking. Asia is on America's doorstep—not just economically but spiritually as well. Moreover, a careful reading of the biblical account in Genesis of the temptation in the Garden of Eden reveals the way New Age activities simply represent the never-ending attempt by the Tempter to convince man he can be a god.

Although New Age origins lie in the ancient Middle East and Asia, one can readily discern certain decades in recent history when Eastern philosophy carved inroads into Western thinking. Within the twentieth century, such points of East-West contact gave birth to what is now referred to as the "New Age Movement." Today, with the application of high technology and speed of communications, New Age influence has infiltrated every area of public life.

However, in a larger sense, the New Age Movement may be viewed as part of a significant shift in worldview on the part of persons living in the United States, Canada, Australia, and Western Europe. As much as 20 percent of the population of these areas has gradually shifted its personal belief system from a Western worldview, based upon certain Judeo-Christian principles, to an Eastern worldview heavily influenced by Eastern religions such as Hinduism and Buddhism. Implications of this changing worldview are enormous, particularly in major Western institutions such as government, education, and the arts.

Such a trend influences the way God is perceived, history is viewed, absolute standards are observed, and human beings are valued. Christians need be both informed and concerned about this significant trend.

But, as this book will point out, Christians need not despair at the spreading influence of the New Age. Not only does the New Age Movement represent fulfillment of certain biblical prophecies concerning the last days but it also presents a challenge to Christians for a strong personal commitment to Jesus Christ as well as an opportunity to respond with boldness and concern for those involved in the New Age Movement. Christians may feel confident in the knowledge that Christ triumphed at Calvary and that, no matter how formidable New Age activities might seem, the Kingdom of Light will be established. Moreover, a great many of those involved in the New Age are genuine seekers of truth with whom Christians have an opportunity to compassionately share the Good News of Jesus Christ.

This book is designed to present an easily readable, straightforward introduction to New Age thinking for the Christian reader who has little previous information concerning this timely subject. Numerous Christian books have been written about the New Age and serve the vital purpose of keeping Christians informed. Many are quite detailed or give personal accounts of experiences of Christians formerly involved in the New Age but can serve as further reading for those who desire more information.

With these thoughts as a point of departure, let us now consider the terminology and definitions found in New Age vocabulary.

2
Defining Our Terms

"I've heard of it, but I'm not exactly sure what it is." That response represents a common answer among Christians when asked the question, "Have you ever heard of the New Age?" Several years ago, the response might well have been, "I've never heard of it." Now the time has come for Christians to move into a greater degree of awareness than a simple familiarity with the term.

Essentially, as used by its adherents, the term *New Age* is a reference to a particular time in the near future when mankind will presumably enter into an era of spiritual enlightenment characterized by the collective realization of the "god-consciousness" within each person. This universal release of such spiritual power will then usher in a "new age" when all mankind will be unified under one government, one religion, and one leader. As a prelude to that particular era, a host of activities, practices, organizations, and communications now exist and may be referred

18

to in a broad sense as the "New Age Movement." The movement serves to build a foundation and to prepare the way for the dawning of that "new age."

Supporters of the New Age sometimes use other terms interchangeably to refer to the same set of principles and beliefs, particularly as New Agers recognize that Christians are becoming more aware of the term *New Age* and thus are encountering Christian opposition. Among the alternative terms are *Human Potential Movement*, the *Aquarian Conspiracy*, the *Age of Aquarius*, the *Third Force*, the *New Spirituality*, and the *New Consciousness*. Each refers to a gradual and, adherents believe, inevitable shift in worldview toward collective god-consciousness and the ultimate perfectibility of mankind.

Modern Origins

Although the roots of the New Age are found in antiquity (*see* chapter 3), more modern origins can be traced to the late nineteenth century in the Theosophical Society founded in New York in 1875 by Helena Petrovna Blavatsky. Drawing upon the Hindu sacred scriptures, the Theosophical Society promoted three specific beliefs: God is impersonal, Jesus was not divine, and human souls are transmigrated.

After Blavatsky's death in 1891, the society continued under the leadership of Annie Besant and eventually passed into the hands of British-born Alice Bailey, an Episcopalian who later settled in California. By the time of her death in 1949, Bailey had broken with the Theosophical Society but had attracted numerous followers and authored many books, including the two-volume *Discipleship*

in the New Age. Bailey's work served not only to join Eastern philosophy with that of the West but also to set modern foundations for what is now called the New Age
Movement. Not only was Bailey quite possibly the first to
have used the term *New Age* but her books also form part
of what may be considered basic doctrine of the New Age.

Other books which also explain the goals and philosophy of the New Age include those of David Spangler and
Marilyn Ferguson. Spangler's *Revelation: the Birth of a New
Age* comes as close to being the "bible" of the New Age as
any other work. Closely akin to Spangler's work is Marilyn Ferguson's *The Aquarian Conspiracy* which, when it appeared in 1980, was guaranteed success by being chosen
as a Book-of-the Month Club selection.

Both Spangler and Ferguson envision a coming era
when a global change will take place to release full human
potential and usher in an age of universal peace and harmony. From the foundational New Age writings of these
and other authors, certain basic principles can be discerned which characterize almost all aspects of the New
Age Movement.

Monism

The first distinctive element of New Age thinking is
what is referred to as *monism.* This is the belief that "all is
one and one is all." Monism abandons the concept of the
individual self, created in the image of a living God, and
substitutes a "universal self" in which all living beings—
past, present, and future—are blended together. Thus the
term *the One* becomes a definition of all selves united into
one. Diversity becomes unity—a very Hindu concept.

Taken a step further, monism leads to the ultimate claim that man is God. This concept of the "divine within" comprises a central and almost universally held principle of New Age followers. The "divine within" not only lowers God and elevates mankind but actually goes a step further by merging the two. Whereas humanism, as defined by the Greeks and later by Renaissance philosophers, declared that man is the measure of all things and therefore really doesn't need a personal God, the New Age goes on to suggest that man actually *is* God. The realization of this god-consciousness comprises one of the major goals of the New Age Movement because of the conviction that the collective realization by all mankind will usher in the predicted "new age."

The "divine within" concept that says we are all gods is antithetical to everything biblical Christianity represents. The thread running throughout the Bible from Genesis to Revelation is that God, the Creator, while loving and personal, is yet sovereign and separate from His creation. Genesis 1:27 records the ultimate act of the divine Creator: "So God created man in his own image, in the image of God he created him; male and female he created them." This unique creation does not, however, imply that man is God any more than a child who resembles his father *is* his father; the two are still separate entities.

Moreover, the concept of the "divine within" eliminates one of the most profound teachings of the Bible: Man was created to have a relationship with God. To think that man, with all of his frailties and mistakes, can yet have a living relationship with the holy God of the universe, is not only an explosive concept but life-changing as well. That is exactly the overwhelming message that Jesus brought to mankind. He came to reveal the Fatherheart of God and to show the Father's eternal love for mankind by providing redemption through His own sacrifice on the cross. To merge the Creator with the created, as monism suggests, is to deprive a human being of the most meaningful and fulfilling of earthly possibilities: a personal and even intimate relationship with God the Father. Man, the created, reaches his highest potential when he enters into the fullness of that relationship with God, the Creator, and thus receives all that human-divine relationship can provide. This is the heart of Christianity.

Not only does monism suggest the "divine within" but also the "divine without"; that is, God is not only in us, He also is in everything else. Herein lies the essence of pantheism, the suggestion that God can be found in such places as trees, rocks, sunsets, the Grand Canyon, and the Big Dipper. Certainly the infinitely imaginative mind of the Creator can be seen in all of nature from spiderwebs to galaxies, but the essential difference still exists: the created is not the Creator. The Apostle Paul warned against pantheism in Romans 1:25: "They exchanged the truth of God for a lie, and worshiped and served created things rather than the Creator—who is forever praised. Amen." Thus Paul makes clear that, while God is the Creator, we cannot worship Him by worshiping the things He created.

Syncretism

This concept of monism leads naturally to the second very important principle of the New Age Movement: All religions are one. Consequently, New Age thinking has become a spiritual smorgasbord of ideas and thoughts ranging from Hinduism, Buddhism, Taoism, and mysticism to Gnosticism and humanism. This mixture of religions, known as *syncretism*, suggests that all religions are really leading to the same goal and thus everyone will eventually arrive at the same spiritual destination or, as a Japanese proverb suggests, "Many paths lead up Mount Fuji but all arrive at the top."

Not only does syncretism provide a smorgasbord of spiritual tenets but it also allows each individual to devise his own set of religious beliefs to fit his own needs and, more importantly, to justify his own behavior. Thus behavior becomes relative: nothing can be called right or wrong. What is evil to one person can be good for another and vice versa. "To each his own" becomes a casual rationalization for all human behavior, including issues involving the sanctity of human life such as abortion and euthanasia. The Bible clearly warns us of such moral justification in Isaiah 5:20, 21: "Woe to those who call evil good and good evil, who put darkness for light and light for darkness, who put bitter for sweet and sweet for bitter. Woe to those who are wise in their own eyes and clever in their own sight."

Of course, syncretism also eliminates the need to face up to the problem of sin because one can choose religious beliefs that do not remind one of the issue of personal sin—that which separates us from a holy and perfect God. If evil can become good and good can become evil, nothing can be labeled as sin. Taken a step futher, this means that the atoning sacrifice of Jesus Christ on the cross of Calvary was unnecessary. The messianic theme of the Bible is that God, in His fathomless love and boundless desire to redeem mankind, would send a Messiah who would save His people from their sins. The Judeo-Christian concept of sin called for a blood sacrifice in order to first provide forgiveness from a holy, perfect God, thereby opening the way for a relationship with God. Second, the sacrifice was to relieve mankind from the devastating burden of personal guilt for sin. The summation of the biblical theme is simply stated in Romans 3:23, 24: "For all have sinned and fall short of the glory of God, and are justified freely by his grace through the redemption that came by Christ Jesus."

Interestingly, Dr. Karl Menninger, modern pioneer in treatment of the mentally ill, suggested in his book *Whatever Became of Sin?* that personal guilt for unrecognized and unconfessed sin is responsible for a considerable amount of mental illness.[1] Unfortunately, New Age thinking not only denies the existence of personal sin but consequently leaves its adherents with the burden, even if unexpressed, of guilt from those sins. Thus, although many may give lip service to having found the answer to their spiritual quest in the New Age Movement, the nagging problem of personal sin remains because it can only be solved God's way—through the atonement of His Son, Jesus Christ.

Rejection of the Deity of Jesus Christ

Closely related to the concept of syncretism is the rejection of the deity of Jesus Christ. Central to New Age thinking is the demotion of Jesus Christ from His divinity as Immanuel, "God with us," to simply being a man with all of the accompanying weaknesses of manhood. If the New Age can reduce Jesus to the status of any other human being and thus deprive Him of His essential divinity, then His death on the cross becomes meaningless and all of His exclusive claims about Himself rejected.

To New Agers, one of the most objectionable of Jesus' claims was His exclusive and profound claim recorded in John 14:6: "I am the way and the truth and the life. No one comes to the Father except through me." Jesus' claims were so exclusive and unprecedented that they must be dealt with. Either He was exactly who He said He was or He was nothing at all; there is no middle ground. But New Agers reject the suggestion of only one way and, in keeping with principles of syncretism, claim that there are many ways to the truth.

What the New Age Movement has done with Jesus is place Him in the human company of other religious leaders such as Buddha, Lao-tzu, Moses, Elijah, and Muhammad. New Agers have not rejected Jesus' existence; they have simply demoted Him. Using confusing terminology, New Age philosophy is rife with references to "the Christ" or "the Cosmic Christ." None of these is the Jesus Christ of the New Testament. Rather, to New Agers, these Christs are "God incarnated" at any given time in history. As will be shown in a subsequent chapter, many New Agers are now eagerly awaiting the appearance of Lord Maitreya, whom they believe to be the greatest of the Cosmic Christs.

But such claims should not be surprising to Christians. Jesus Himself warned that false Christs would come. In Matthew 24:23, 24 Jesus proclaimed, "At that time if anyone says to you, 'Look, here is the Christ!' or, 'There he is!' do not believe it. For false Christs and false prophets will appear and perform great signs and miracles to deceive even the elect—if that were possible." In 1 John 4:1–3 we are told that any spirit that denies Jesus is not from God and is, in fact, the spirit of the antichrist.

Not only does New Age philosophy reject the deity of Jesus Christ but many New Agers are adamantly opposed to the concept of monotheism, which is the belief in only one God. Humans cannot be elevated to god positions if there is only one God. Thus Judaism, Christianity, and Islam, the three great monotheistic religions of the world, are anathema to such New Agers. Rather, New Age belief substitutes the impersonal concept of an "Absolute Entity" or a "Cosmic Mind" from which all persons may tap wisdom and into which all persons may someday merge.

Self-Deification

If every person can be his or her own god, then the deification of self naturally follows. A great number of New Age activities are designed to achieve "self-fulfillment" or "self-actualization." Thus the term *Human Potential Movement* has sometimes been used interchangeably with the term *New Age*.

While the desire to "fulfill self" seems like a very attractive goal and one which would bring happiness, the term is actually quite deceptive. The problem lies not in the desire to be happy and to achieve success, goals common to all mankind, but in the methods employed for the attainment of such goals. New Age methods for self-actualization encourage one to *turn inward* for the answers, for guidance and wisdom. This does not mean quieting oneself in order to hear the voice of God, as Christians are encouraged to do. Rather, this New Age principle suggests that because each person *is* God, each person has the answers within him and need look no further. The center of one's existence becomes the self, which is a very small and fallible world indeed.

Thus New Age teaching suggests that each person needs no one else, exists sufficient unto himself, has intrinsic power, and can find the way to self-improvement within his own capacities. Meditation, one of the most common New Age activities, encourages concentration on the "light within" and turning one's thoughts inward to discover one's own "energy source." The deep introspection that accompanies such attempts at self-improvement and self-actualization leads to enthronement of self and self-idolatry.

The Bible warns against the fallacy of looking to ourselves for answers to our own problems. In Mark 7:20–23 Jesus warned, "What comes out of a man is what makes him 'unclean.' For from within, out of men's hearts, come evil thoughts, sexual immorality, theft, murder, adultery, greed, malice, deceit, lewdness, envy, slander, arrogance, and folly. All these evils come from inside and make a man 'unclean.' " Likewise Jeremiah 17:9 reminds us of the deceitfulness of our own hearts: "The heart is deceitful above all things and beyond cure. Who can understand it?" While meditation is referred to in the Bible, the object of that meditation is not the self but quite the opposite. Psalm 1:2, one of the many verses in the Psalms in which David refers to meditation, says, "But his delight is in the law of the Lord, and on his law he meditates day and night."

Reincarnation

Because of the strong emphasis upon self-fulfillment found in New Age thinking, the belief in reincarnation is also commonly held by many New Agers. The burden of failure to reach self-actualization in one's present life lifts when the suggestion is offered that one may have many more lives in which to achieve such full human potential Moreover, disappointments and tragedies of this life can be explained as the result of Karma, the companion belief of reincarnation.

The Law of Karma, the universal law of cause and effect, suggests that whatever happens in one's present life results from actions taken in the previous life. Hence, the nature of the next life can be predetermined by actions taken in this life. Thus the ultimate New Age goal of achieving god-consciousness may require many incarnations, thereby shifting the burden of ultimate success to the efforts of each person alone and with no guarantee of success.

The belief in reincarnation and the ultimate goal of the perfectibility of all mankind provides the framework within which to advocate the belief in evolution. Mankind's course through the millennia is simply seen as a forward march in which human beings evolve toward flawless excellence. Ultimately, according to New Age adherents, a race of superhumans must be created who, because of their collective god-consciousness, will rule the universe.

From a Christian perspective, the belief in reincarnation conflicts with biblical teaching. At no point does either Old or New Testament teaching substantiate the concept of reincarnation. Hebrews 9:27 states unequivocally, "Man is destined to die once, and after that to face judgment."

One World Government

Finally, because of the New Age goal for universal peace and harmony achieved through collective god-consciousness, the concept of one world government is also commonly held by New Age adherents Such terms as *global initiative* and *planetary healing* embody the one-world principle. Eventually such a world government, according to its supporters, would encompass every facet of human endeavor from family life and education to finance and defense. For many who subscribe to the one-world concept, the United Nations and its subsidiary activities and organizations represent a beginning point for the accomplishment of such a scenario.

Because of its all-encompassing nature, one world government would be antithetical to biblical teaching. One world government demands a leader or body of leaders to whom all peoples of the world would be asked to give obedience. During the temptation in the desert, Jesus Himself rejected just such an enticing offer from Satan with the words that still stand true today. "Worship the Lord your God, and serve him only" (Matthew 4:10).

While the Apostle Paul reminds us that "everyone must submit himself to the governing authorities, for there is no authority except that which God has established" (Romans 13:1), the suggestion of a universal government ruled by a single person claiming to be a god leads to idolatry, the great sin of Israel punishable by a jealous God. Only One will rule over all the earth, the One spoken of in Revelation 1:5. "Jesus Christ, who is the faithful witness, the firstborn from the dead, and the ruler of the kings of the earth " Jesus Christ's kingdom, prophesied in Revelation, truly represents the triumph of good over evil.

Thus, we can conclude that although the New Age Movement encompasses a variety of activities, certain common themes can be identified: the insistence that every person is his own god; the syncretic belief that all religions are leading to the same goal; the denial of the deity of Jesus Christ; the search for self-realization and self-empowerment; the personal acceptance of the doctrine of reincarnation; and the goal of one world government under one world leader. All of these form the foundation for the New Age Movement. Because of their importance, several will be discussed at greater length in subsequent chapters. But first let us consider the roots of the New Age Movement.

II

WHERE DID IT COME FROM?

3
Back to the Roots

In his great wisdom, King Solomon wrote, "What has been will be again, what has been done will be done again; there is nothing new under the sun" (Ecclesiastes 1:9). Certainly his statement can be applied to the New Age Movement. The "new" in New Age represents nothing new at all but is as old as the ancient religions from which it forms its root system.

In the Genesis account of the temptation in the Garden of Eden, we see the seeds planted which contain the original lie of Satan: humans can be gods, can obtain all knowledge, and can live forever. The Genesis account of the Great Tempter's enticing statement reads, "For God knows that when you eat of it your eyes will be opened, and you will be like God, knowing good and evil" (3:5). Thus was the spiritual basis for the struggle between the Kingdom of Light and the Kingdom of Darkness established—a struggle which has manifested itself in

33

many religions and philosophies, including the New Age Movement.

The Babylonian Mystery Religion

By the time of Judeo-Christian patriarch Abraham, the Mystery Religion of Babylon, a religion filled with pagan rituals, had established itself in the Mesopotamian region. With its elevation of humans to the status of gods and goddesses, its worship of nature, its divination and occult practices as well as its espousal of reincarnation, the ancient Babylonian religion became a fountainhead from which coursed other religious systems. Its subtle temptations eventually wooed the tribes of Israel away from God into idolatry.

Moreover, the deceptions of the ancient Babylonian Mystery Religion have remained through the millennia and are spoken of in the last-days scenario described in the Book of Revelation. There, the power exerted by the Mystery of Babylon, which is compared with that of a drunken prostitute, is at last ended forever (chapters 17, 18).

Hinduism

Among the ancient religions reflecting the influence of the Babylonian practices is Hinduism. By its own definition "the Mother of Religions," Hinduism provides much of the religious foundation for the other Asian religions of Buddhism, Sikhism, and Jainism, as well as for New Age philosophy.

Although Hindu origins remain somewhat obscure, Sanskrit religious hymns known as the *Vedas* were written down sometime around 1200 B.C. These sacred scriptures, including the *Rigveda* and the *Upanishads*, contain accounts of the gods and goddesses worshiped in this agricultural civilization.

By 500 B.C., the major tenets of Hinduism had taken form. These included the caste system, the belief in reincarnation, and the Doctrine of Karma. As the religion developed, these three Hindu principles became inseparable and interdependent. One's caste is determined by one's karma, which is in turn passed through one incarnation to another. Simply stated, the Law of Karma suggests that whatever happens to a person in this life was predetermined by his actions in the previous life. Therefore nothing can be done to escape one's lot in this life.

Despite this fatalistic view, at the very basis of Hinduism lies the suggestion that man can have anything he wants. Hindu gurus (teachers) feel safe in offering such a tantalizing prospect in the firm belief that eventually every person will renounce what he thought would make him happy (the Path of Renunciation) and will opt for a search for that which man truly wants. What man truly wants, suggest Hindu sages, is infinite knowledge, infinite pleasure, and infinite life. Interestingly, these three "wants" correspond to the trees described in the Garden of Eden. (*See* Genesis 2, 3.) In other words, man wants to be like God. These three principles take on new importance in the light of present-day New Age thinking.

Like its New Age offspring, Hinduism suggests that every human being already has "god within." The *atman*, or universal soul, can merge with Brahman, the Absolute, and thus obtain release into the infinite. Unlike the God of the Bible who is both infinite and personal, the Absolute

35

(Brahman) of Hinduism combines a mystical merger of both finite and infinite but remains impersonal. Thus Hinduism presents a pantheon of over 330 million gods and goddesses in various incarnations of the Absolute. The goal of a Hindu is to achieve *moksa*, or the release from the cycle of karma and its journey of reincarnations into oneness with the Absolute. There at last desires will be satisfied and godlike status will be achieved.

However, the problem lies in achieving such a goal. The Hindu answer is the path of *yoga*. Millions of Westerners innocently practice various forms of yoga without knowledge of the inseparable connection between the *asanas* (positions) and the religion which created them. For the Hindu, the path of yoga may include *jnana yoga* (seeking God intellectually), *karma yoga* (seeking God through works), *bhakti yoga* (seeking God through devotion), *raja yoga* (seeking God through body and mind control), and *hatha yoga* (seeking God through release of bodily energies). Thus Hinduism becomes individualistic, a religion of works, and a path along which the follower has no guarantee of his own salvation or release from the oppressive Law of Karma.

India, a nation blessed with great physical beauty and abundant human resources, also struggles against grinding poverty, human underdevelopment, and staggering problems for which Hinduism offers few answers except escape into the Path of Renunciation, whereby the devotee renounces all worldly associations. Westerners, seduced by the subtle and lofty tenets of Hinduism, rarely see the dark underside of India, a nation which Indian writer V. S. Naipaul referred to as a "Wounded Civilization."[1] Instead, as we shall see in the next chapter,

Western arms embrace the ancient Hindu beliefs in the misplaced hope that somehow Hinduism offers answers to complex Western problems.

Buddhism

Another religious influence on New Age thinking is Buddhism, particularly that of the Zen sect. Buddhism, which represents a "reformation" of Hinduism, traces its origin to the sixth century B.C. and Siddhartha Gautama, a Nepalese prince whose rejection of court life led him on a lifelong search for spiritual enlightenment. Following various phases, including severe fasting and asceticism, he entered a long meditation under a tree near Banares and, according to Buddhist tradition, received a flash of enlightenment. Henceforth known as the Buddha (Enlightened One), he traveled about teaching his new religion.

Although maintaining the Hindu concept of reincarnation, Buddhism rejects much of the ritualism and mysticism of Hinduism. At the foundation of Buddhism rests the belief that all of life consists of suffering brought on by one's selfish desire. According to Buddhists, such selfish desire can and must be overcome—an action which releases the follower into *nirvana*, a state of spiritual enlightenment. The method selected for this spiritual journey, known as the Eightfold Path, consists largely of moral and behavioral rules which have had a profound cultural effect on Southeast and East Asia. Correct speech, correct behavior, correct mindfulness, correct meditation, and correct effort comprise some of the Eightfold Path. Like Hinduism, Buddhism is a religion of works, meaning each believer must achieve nirvana on his own with no guarantee of success.

As Buddhism made its way into China, then to Korea and Japan, a meditative sect developed. This sect became known as Ch'an in China and Zen in Japan. A particularly popular religion during the samurai era of Japanese history, Zen followers adhered to a strict life-style of meditation and spartan living.

With its emphasis on mind control and self-discipline, the heart of Zen practice remains that of meditation, often concentrating on a *koan*, or problem. Because of its emphasis on a simpler life-style and meditation, Zen has attracted many followers in the West who want to retreat from the fast lane of modern life. Thus, with its support for reincarnation, mind control, meditation, and spiritual enlightenment, Buddhism can be described as yet another of the roots for the New Age Movement.

Taoism

Although Taoism (pronounced "dowism") usually falls into the category of a philosophy rather than that of a religion, certain Taoist influences can be seen in New Age philosophy. Begun in China sometime during the sixth century B.C. by a mystical figure, Lao-tzu, Taoist principles gradually permeated all of East Asian culture from Korea to Singapore and from Taiwan to Hong Kong. Even today, as the Pacific Rim nations move into high-tech modernization, Taoist influence remains in many subtle ways.

The heart of Taoist teaching insists that "Tao," an unexplainable but pervasive life-giving entity, exists in all things. Tao, this first principle of all being, forms the basis of the universe and is timeless and indescribable. Qualities emphasized by Taoists such as humility, noncompetition, and simplicity are still in evidence in East Asian culture. As it developed, Taoism also became pantheistic, with an emphasis upon harmony with nature (an influence which can be seen in Chinese landscape paintings)

But perhaps the most important influence of Taoism, and one which can be discerned in New Age philosophy, is the concept of *yin and yang*. Although the yin and yang principle probably predated Taoism, it became a major part of Taoist teaching. According to this tenet, all things are constantly changing, a process represented by the existence of yin and yang in all things. Yin becomes yang and yang becomes yin. For example, cold becomes hot, dark becomes light, winter becomes summer, etc. This principle is symbolized by an *s*-shaped swirl within a circle, a commonly seen symbol in East Asia.

The yin/yang concept suggests that nothing is absolute: all things are relative. For example, good can become evil and evil can become good. The two simply balance each other rather than exist as opposites or absolutes. Such a belief, when adopted into one's personal set of ethics and morality, can be used to justify any behavior. This method of relative thinking has taken on new meaning in the West as it can now be seen in New Age ethics.

But a biblical perspective firmly rejects such relative thinking. God is a God of absolutes. In Malachi 3:6, the Creator of the universe states categorically, "I am the Lord, I change not" (KJV). In the New Testament, James 1:17, God is presented as unchangeable and as the representation of all that is perfect. We read, "Every good and perfect gift is from above, coming down from the Father of the heavenly lights, who does not change like shifting shadows "

One of the many characteristics that separate the God of the Bible from all others is that He is absolute. When each person becomes his own god, as the New Age suggests, the standards from which behavior is measured become not only relative but unpredictable as well. What can be trusted today can be doubted tomorrow Life loses its sacred meaning. In such a world of relative ethics, nothing stands in the way of people turning upon each other and ultimately destroying themselves

Gnosticism

Finally, in tracing the complex religious and philosophical root system of the New Age Movement, we must consider the second-century A.D. Christian heresy known as Gnosticism. Taking its name from the Greek word *gnosis*, meaning "esoteric knowledge," Gnosticism represents a syncretistic set of beliefs that originated in ancient Mesopotamia, Egypt, and India. These beliefs found their way into Western thinking during the Greco-Roman period.

Gnostics suggested that every person has within him a divine "spark of life" that can be awakened only through esoteric knowledge. The world, according to Gnostics, represents an evil place in which man's salvation and escape from evil can be accomplished only through knowledge. When such exclusive knowledge is attained, the divine spark ignites and the person can merge with the divine.

Furthermore, Gnostics concluded, Jesus was one of those "Christs" who came to reveal knowledge and mysteries; thus His crucifixion was not a sacrifice since the "spirit of Christ" was lifted from Jesus at the point of His crucifixion Thereafter, according to Gnosticism, Jesus' disciples and other early Christian leaders corrupted Jesus' teachings. Nevertheless, a redeemer figure would provide the saving *gnosis*, or knowledge, for a selected elite. After death, these elite persons pass upward toward unity with the supreme power from which they had originated.

Not surprisingly, early Christian church fathers branded Gnosticism as heresy. To them, Gnosticism not only denied the sacrificial death of Jesus but also belittled the role of faith, replacing faith with esoteric knowledge.

Certainly, the influence of Gnosticism upon today's New Age Movement can be identified. The suggestion of the divine spark within each person, the denial of the sacrificial death of Jesus, the belief that a selected elite can attain unity with a supreme being, and the search for esoteric knowledge all fit comfortably within the tenets of the New Age.

In summation, as one examines the ancient religions from the East, certain themes emerge which can be seen today in the philosophy of the New Age Movement. The Babylonian Mystery Religion not only elevated humans to godlike status but also espoused the doctrine of reincarnation. The belief in reincarnation was then passed on in Hinduism and Buddhism and is a central tenet of New Age thinking. Both Hinduism and Buddhism attached the Law of Karma, the law of cause and effect, to the belief in reincarnation. Today, many New Agers make reference to their "karma."

The central New Age suggestion that every person is part of God and must tap the "divine within" draws heavily from Hinduism. The goal of all Hindus is to achieve oneness with the Absolute, a goal now transplanted to the West. Moreover, meditation and yoga, two practices which are widely exercised among New Agers, also have Hindu roots. Forms of Zen meditation, a Buddhist refinement, still maintain popularity in the West.

Finally, the concept that all things in the universe are relative and constantly changing can be traced to Taoism. Such thinking has been used as a justification for negative human behavior when needed to fit the circumstance. Likewise, the concept of the "divine spark" within each person as well as the denial of the deity and sacrificial death of Jesus Christ can be traced to Gnosticism. Thus the "new" in New Age really represents a modern hybrid of very old concepts.

4
East Meets West

"O East is East and West is West, / And never the twain shall meet." These famous words penned by Rudyard Kipling, poet of the British Empire, have proven inaccurate. In reality, East and West not only have met but they also have courted and married in the form of the New Age Movement.

Even before the time of Christ, trade and cultural contact transpired between the Mediterranean world and the civilizations of Asia. The armies of Alexander the Great marched as far as northern India and not only brought back exotic products but also religious ideas which then found their way into Greek philosophy. Certainly the heresy of Gnosticism, discussed in the previous chapter, reflected the influence of Eastern mysticism.

More recently, in the late 1800s London provided a setting that attracted many persons interested in the occult and Eastern mysticism. The Theosophical Society, founded in 1875, developed into the modern setting for an East-West marriage. Alice Bailey then brought the teachings of the Theosophical Society to the United States during this century.

The 1960s

However, from a contemporary viewpoint, the 1960s, that decade of angry turmoil, laid the modern foundation for the New Age Movement. Historians now refer to the 1960s as the era in which America "came apart." Not only did it appear that the very fabric of American society was ripping apart but television also brought the drama into the nation's living rooms and forever etched unforgettable scenes into the American memory.

When the decade opened with the election of a dashing young president, few could have perceived the turmoil that lay ahead. John F. Kennedy's challenging words, "Ask not what your country can do for you—ask what you can do for your country," eventually became nothing more than an echo to those who would choose to drop out of society and retreat into a counterculture. A decade which inaugurated the Peace Corps in order to encourage selfless devotion to the less fortunate would give way to the "me generation" of the 1970s. What was to have been the New Frontier actually set the stage for the New Age. What went wrong along the way?

Few eras in American history have produced such tumultuous years with such long-lasting influences as the decade of the 1960s. Racial prejudice, long swept under the national carpet, suddenly appeared to a nation that revealed surprisingly vehement opposing emotions in the North as well as in the South. In 1961, blood was shed on the campus of the University of Mississippi when James Meredith, a Black student, tried to enroll in classes. The resulting violence turned out to be the opening salvo for a bloody decade of racial confrontation that would eventually claim the life of its chief spokesperson, Dr. Martin Luther King, Jr. But even as the struggle for racial equality continued, another explosive issue was developing.

In the early years of the decade, few outside of Pentagon circles were aware of the gradual commitment America was making in a faraway spot on the map called Vietnam. Eventually, that Asian name would turn American against American. In reality, the bitterness created by the war in Vietnam was only a symptom of a far deeper American affliction.

A generation of young Americans born after World War II was coming of age in the 1960s. Few of these youth knew anything about economic depression or personal deprivation. The 1950s, boom years in American society, provided the postwar generation with an abundance of material possessions and opportunities for education. Yet a moral and spiritual vacuum prevailed which would manifest itself in an unprecedented fashion in the 1960s.

By 1962, a bushy-haired folksinger named Bob Dylan was becoming the musical mouthpiece for a sizable group of peace activists, antibomb enthusiasts, and other youth disgruntled with society. Dylan, and other folksingers such as Joan Baez, seemed to be voicing the suppressed feelings of many of America's youth. Although a counterculture was being born, mainstream Americans remained blissfully unaware of dark undercurrents developing in their society.

That naivete was shattered on November 22, 1963, a day forever frozen in the minds of Americans old enough to remember the assassination of President Kennedy. Television brought the tragedy into America's living rooms to a stunned people. More than the nation's leader had been lost. An idealistic dream that man could create a better world in which to live also seemed far out of reach.

America's youth turned their eyes elsewhere for answers. In 1964, a few short months after the Kennedy assassination, England exported its most controversial product of the decade: the Beatles. The Western world had never seen anything quite like the frenzy stirred by these four mopheads from Liverpool. By the standards of 1970, the Beatles of 1964, with their short hair and dark suits, seemed innocuous. Their first hits, including the playful "I Want to Hold Your Hand," were a long way from the haunting realities of Paul McCartney's "Let It Be" (1970) or the mystical subtleties of George Harrison's "My Sweet Lord" (1971).

The transformation of the Beatles between 1962 and 1970 served as a reflection of the change taking place in Western society. This change should not be understated because it played a prominent role in laying the modern foundation for the New Age Movement.

The New Left

America's college and university campuses provided the theater for an unfolding drama of the 1960s which eventually produced a full-blown counterculture. Although more of America's youth were receiving the advantage of a college education than ever before, more also seemed dissatisfied with the world in which they lived.

In 1964, the Free Speech Movement began on the campus of the University of California at Berkeley. The movement led to demonstrations, arrests, counterdemonstrations, and a pattern which would spread across the nation's campuses. Mainstream America was shocked at the intensity of rebelliousness exhibited by its youth. Still, Americans turned their backs to the problems. The big movies of the year, *Mary Poppins* and *My Fair Lady*, reflected America's desire to retreat into the world of musical fantasy.

But names like Vietcong, Saigon, and William Westmoreland and words like *escalation* cropped up in America's vocabulary. Gradually more and more of America's young men were off to another war, eventually in numbers that would swell to half a million. Protests mounted. The voice of protest, now known as the New Left, seemed to vent more than just antiwar frustrations. A *generation gap* was the sociologists' term for a host of pent-up frustrations of America's youth against what they called "the Establishment." The Establishment seemed to be anyone over the age of thirty or anything that represented structure or limitations to one's activities. From New York to San Francisco, a generation of young Americans embraced an alternative life-style.

Whether people called them hippies or flower children, their numbers were many. At least ten thousand of them celebrated "flower power" in Central Park on a Sunday afternoon in 1967. A former Harvard professor named Timothy Leary had encouraged them to "tune in, turn on, and drop out" by using a powerful hallucinogenic drug known as LSD. The psychedelic experiences produced by LSD, coupled with an increasing interest in Eastern mysticism and the occult, created two of the most significant aspects of the 1960s counterculture—aspects which would pave the way for the New Age Movement of the 1980s and 1990s.

The volatile combination of hallucinogenic drugs and Eastern mysticism opened a Pandora's box. Curiosity led to experimentalism and this experimentalism, taken to the extreme, resulted in death and destruction. Rock stars Janis Joplin and Jimi Hendrix overdosed on drugs, victims of a counterculture turned ugly. Other victims, not so well known, died in obscurity in the back alleys of Haight-Ashbury or Greenwich Village. Still others permanently damaged their minds in "acid trips" gone wrong. Peace slogans and love beads of the flower children gave way to the hard realities of an uncertain world.

India and the Beatles

If hallucinogenic drugs represented the quick pathway to altered states of consciousness for the counterculture, rock musicians became the gurus who led the way. The Beatles, foremost of the rock musicians, were finding their own guru. Despite their phenomenal worldwide success, the Beatles remained restless and seemingly unfulfilled. In 1967, their search for fulfillment led them to the feet of the Maharishi Mahesh Yogi, a Hindu guru from India. The Maharishi, whose brand of transcendental meditation advanced him all the way to the bank, taught an interesting blend of Western materialism and Eastern mysticism.

The Beatles' trip to India in 1968 marked an important point in the East-West courtship. Overnight, the Maharishi became a celebrity, transcendental meditation (TM) caught on, and other Indian gurus gradually made their way to the West, bringing with them their adaptable forms of Hinduism. For a generation of young people, disillusioned by the assassinations of political leaders, angered by the Vietnam War, and frustrated by environmental and societal problems, the new spiritualism offered a tantalizing alternative. In increasing numbers, American and West European youth trekked through India and Nepal seeking to fill a spiritual vacuum in their lives.

Gradually, new words crept into America's vocabulary A movie star talked about his "karma." A college roommate was studying "Zen." Over a cup of herbal tea, two women in their late twenties could be heard talking about their "mantras." New stores, often clustered near university campuses, featured vegetarian foods, incense sticks, Hindu sacred scriptures, and imported cotton clothing made in India. One could wander into a bookstore, often greeted by the sweet aroma of marijuana, and browse through shelves of how-to books—how to teach yourself Zen meditation, how to learn yoga exercises, and how to prepare foods macrobiotically. The East had not only met the West but had become financially profitable as well.

Not only did rock musicians turn their faces Eastward but Broadway also joined the trend. In 1968, the highly controversial musical *Hair* opened on Broadway. While the play featured an anti-Establishment theme of the flower children, the most memorable offering was the presentation of nudity on the live stage. *Hair* eventually ran 1,750 performances on Broadway and toured the rest of America, Canada, and West Europe, grossing $80 million. Significantly, a haunting melody from the musical caught on across America's airwaves. "This is the dawning of the Age of Aquarius," the chorus sang, often joined by the audience. The words were prophetic. The use of the astrological term was no coincidence and indicated the degree of occult influence on America's counterculture.

The importance of the 1960s in laying the groundwork for the New Age Movement should not be understated. While the hippie movement passed, the spiritual influence of the East made its way into mainstream Western culture during the 1970s and 1980s. Herein lies the most important single aspect of the counterculture's flirtation with Eastern mysticism: it did not go away but simply took on new but subtle and powerful forms.

Many of yesterday's flower children are today's "yuppies." Love beads have given way to Rolex watches; Indian cotton has given way to designer suits. Psychedelically painted Volkswagen vans have given way to BMWs. But the spiritual search goes on. Those who once sat cross-legged, smoking marijuana and listening to Ravi Shankar play his sitar at Woodstock, may now attend corporate seminars designed to teach employees how to reach full human potential through mind control. While the counterculture of the 1960s represented a certain minority segment of the population, today's New Age Movement, with its many subtleties, is rapidly becoming an integrated part of prevailing Western culture.

5
Toward the Age of Aquarius

First sung in 1968 in the musical *Hair*, the enticing words, "This is the dawning of the Age of Aquarius" issued the clarion call for the New Age. According to leaders of the New Age Movement, the New Age will be the Age of Aquarius. In astrological terms, the Aquarian Age will begin when a shift occurs in the vernal equinox, a shift which some believe took place on December 31, 1986. Others believe such an astrological shift has yet to take place at the turn of the century when the vernal equinox will pass from Pisces, the Fishes, to Aquarius, the Water Bearer. New Agers suggest that such an event will signal the end of the Christian Age (interestingly, the fish was a symbol of early Christianity) and usher in a new spirit symbolized by Aquarius, the Water Bearer, pouring water over the whole planet. Consequently a new age will be inaugurated in which the planet will be healed and personal problems will disappear—submerged into a great cosmic consciousness.

But how is such an Age of Aquarius to be implemented? Does some blueprint exist espoused by New Agers, or is this era to evolve inevitably from a natural set of circumstances? While many hundreds of thousands of persons are involved in the New Age Movement without realizing the immensity of what they are involved in (*see* chapter 6), the leadership of the New Age fully acknowledge the existence of what is, by their own admission, "the Plan."

Before considering the major aspects of the Plan, a legitimate question might be posed: Is the New Age Movement a conspiracy? The answer is not quite so simple as one might think. History abounds with conspiracy theories, whether they are to explain the assassinations of Abraham Lincoln and John F. Kennedy or the bombing of Pearl Harbor. The term *conspiracy* suggests mental images of secret coordination, sinister plots, and some kind of central planning carried on behind closed doors. Therein lies the dilemma of seeing the New Age Movement as a conspiracy. Where is the control room? Who is in charge? Who makes the plans and carries them out?

These factors notwithstanding, in a universal sense, unparalleled in history, the New Age Movement can be viewed as a conspiracy—a conspiracy of eternal and global proportions. The New Age Movement must be understood as a viable contemporary component of Satan's plan—a plan existing since the moment of Satan's (then called Lucifer) expulsion from heaven at some point in the eons of time past. From that cataclysmic event, the Kingdom of Darkness has been arrayed against the Kingdom of Light in a battle for the eternal destinies of human beings. The New Age Movement must be viewed as a compelling force in that titanic struggle in which Satan is determined to defeat the kingdom of Jesus Christ.

Furthermore, ten or fifteen years ago an observer might not have thought of asking whether the New Age Movement incorporated some kind of overall plan. Not only was the term *New Age* rarely used but its activities were not widespread or openly seen. Today, with the increased visibility of the New Age Movement, the question concerning some kind of coordinated plan is a legitimate one.

The Plan

This fact leads back to what some New Age leaders openly refer to as "the Plan." Even in the 1940s, Alice Bailey spoke of implementation of the Plan based upon instructions which she reportedly received from a Tibetan spirit medium. The Plan proposed to usher in a new world order which is, of course, the very heart of the Age of Aquarius. This new world order calls for unity of all peoples everywhere. Every aspect of society from government to religion to the arts and sciences would be unified in order to serve the cause of hastening mankind toward godhood status.

In order to accomplish this unity, according to the Plan, three ideals are necessary: one world government, one world leader, and one world religion. Although the ultimate goal is world domination, such global unity will, by necessity, transpire in stages. According to those who espouse the Plan, intermediate steps involving economic, social, and political changes must be implemented.

For example, in the economic arena, a global control system for food distribution would be instituted as well as a universal credit card which would be necessary for buying or selling. The use of the universal credit card would require each person in the world to have a number so that eventually currency as we know it today would no longer be necessary.

Politically, national boundaries would be erased, along with individual and sovereign governments. The concepts of nationalism and patriotism to one's own country would be discouraged and ultimately obliterated. The superpowers would be replaced by a single "suprapower."

In keeping with this global theme, a recent full-page message paid for by the members of the World Federalist Association in honor of their president, Norman Cousins, appeared in the widely circulated newspaper *The Christian Science Monitor*. The bold headlines state, "World Peace Through World Law, an Idea Whose Time Is Coming!" The announcement congratulates world leaders for their contributions toward world federalism and concludes with the statement by Norman Cousins, "A new world is waiting to be born."[1] Such an announcement may be another indication to Christians of the trend in the world today toward fulfillment of biblical prophecies regarding the way a single world government will not only become acceptable but even eagerly awaited.

Lord Maitreya

Moreover, such a single world government calls for a single world leader—one of the central features of the Plan. Some New Agers, such as spokesperson Benjamin

Creme, believe this single world leader is already alive and about to reveal himself as Lord Maitreya.[2] New Agers suggest that to Jews, he is the longed-for Messiah; to Christians, he is the Christ coming a second time; to Buddhists, he is the Fifth Buddha; to Muslims, he is the Imam Mahdi; and to Hindus, he is Krishna reincarnated.

Whatever the world calls him, New Age leaders believe Lord Maitreya will lead the world into a new era of peace. Lord Maitreya's advance man, the soft-spoken British artist Benjamin Creme, declared that Lord Maitreya presently lives in London and will soon publicly proclaim himself the new world leader. Consequently, the first eye-catching announcement was placed in leading newspapers and magazines in the United States and Western Europe. On Monday, January 12, 1987, the announcement appeared in the widely circulated newspaper *USA Today*. In large letters, the ad boldly stated, "The Christ Is in the World." Other statements went on to describe this Christ as "a great World Teacher for people of every religion and no religion. A practical man with solutions to our problems. He loves ALL humanity." The fine print quoted the Christ as offering "the way forward into a simpler life." This new era for mankind would offer "Sharing and Justice, Brotherhood and Freedom." He then promised to "reveal Myself at the earliest possible moment and to come before the world as your Friend and Teacher."

According to the Tara Center of North Hollywood, California, which jointly sponsored the announcement, Lord Maitreya has been in a process of emerging onto the world scene since 1977, when he reportedly moved from Pakistan to London. This great world leader will use television to communicate telepathically from his mind to the minds of the entire global population. In late 1988, the erstwhile Creme reviewed the world political situation and predicted that the Day of Declaration was near.

Then, in early April 1990, an advertisement sponsored by the Tara Center announced that an historic global meeting was about to take place in which Lord Maitreya would present his credentials as a world teacher. The announcement declared that the "global transformation" taking place in the world is the result of the presence of Maitreya and that he had already predicted such events as the release of Nelson Mandela, the fall of totalitarian governments, and the global reduction in armaments. Again the announcement suggested that the day of Lord Maitreya's revelation of his true status is not far off.

The coming of a messianic figure not only portends political consequences but religious ones as well. The principle of a one-world religion represents the third central tenet of the Plan proposed by New Age leaders. Actually, the New Age Movement itself is very quickly taking on characteristics of being a religion and, if its leaders were to have their way, would become the universal religion.

Not only does the New Age Movement proffer its messianic figure in the form of Lord Maitreya but it also sets forth sacred books or "bibles." Among others, these include David Spangler's *Reflections of the Christ* and *Revelation: The Birth of a New Age*, Marilyn Ferguson's *The Aquarian Conspiracy*, Alice Bailey's *The Reappearance of the Christ*, and Lola Davis' *Toward a World Religion for a New Age*. These authors join other well-known leaders such as Robert Muller, John Randolph Price, Benjamin Creme, and Vera Alder as the gurus and priests of the New Age.

In addition to its leadership and sacred books, the New Age religion embraces a common spiritual experience or "moment of enlightenment" which serves to tie together a great variety of adherents whose activities seem otherwise unrelated. In order to gain such a spiritual experience, an array of techniques may be used including meditation, yoga, hallucinogenic drugs, channeling, or a variety of other methods. Such a spiritual experience, directed toward developing one's own divinity and expanding one's consciousness, represents the common denominator of New Age followers. This fact represents a key to understanding the rapid spread of New Age influence. From a Christian perspective, this spiritual experience with which so many New Agers identify is in fact a counterfeit religious experience, a topic which will be discussed at greater length in the next chapter.

And what of a Godhead? Since, in New Age thinking, each person is on his way to personal discovery of the "god within," the concept of a single God must be replaced with something far less precise. A variety of terms is used for such a spiritual being: "the Force," "the God of Force," "the Absolute," or "God Transcendent." Such references abandon the Judeo-Christian concept of God as both infinite and personal, a creative God who is sovereign yet unceasingly interested in the lives of individual human beings.

The Great Invocation

Not only has the New Age Movement encouraged religious experiences and ordained individuals to become their own gods but it has also set forth a world prayer which expresses the universality of all religions—a necessary precursor if one world religion is to be established. Known as the Great Invocation, the prayer was first issued in 1945 and has since been used daily by millions of persons worldwide. Hailed by New Age leaders as an expression of unity that will lead the world into the Age of Aquarius, the Great Invocation has been translated into at least fifty languages. Relatively short but very significant in its wording, the Great Invocation is as follows:

> From the point of Light within the Mind of God
> Let light stream forth into the minds of men.
> Let Light descend on Earth.
>
> From the point of Love within the Heart of God
> Let love stream forth into the hearts of men.
> May Christ return to Earth.
>
> From the centre where the Will of God is known
> Let purpose guide the little wills of men—
> The purpose which the Masters know and serve.
>
> From the centre which we call the race of men
> Let the Plan of Love and Light work out.
> And may it seal the door where evil dwells.
> Let Light and Love and Power restore the Plan
> on Earth.[3]

Thus the Great Invocation represents a call for light and love to guide the world—very lofty goals. But what is wrong with the Great Invocation? From a biblical perspective, such a prayer skirts the central theme of the Bible—

that God Himself is love and that His great love is personified in His Son, Jesus Christ, who died that men might live eternally. "The Christ" referred to in the Great Invocation is not the Jesus Christ of the Bible but rather a coming messianic figure (possibly Lord Maitreya) who will rule the world. "The Masters" referred to in the third verse are many and ongoing, of which Jesus Christ is considered only one.

However, the central theme of the Great Invocation is syncretic, that is, all religions are really one and can be unified in such a way as to lead all men to the same spiritual destination. Such syncretism remains antithetical to the biblical teaching that belief in Jesus Christ is the exclusive pathway to God the Father. Jesus proclaimed, "I am the way and the truth and the life. No one comes to the Father except through me" (John 14:6). A lifetime of daily recitation of the Great Invocation as the center of one's prayer life may still leave one empty of the reality of personal salvation and missing the joy of intimate friendship with God.

Networking

If, in fact, the New Age has a plan, how is the word to be spread? The answer lies in an intricate system of networking. By the mid 1980s, linkage and cooperation began to occur between organizations and groups that shared the common goals of the New Age. Quite simply, networking, a key term in New Age vocabulary, represents a crucial element to the implementation of the Age of Aquarius.

In her book *The Aquarian Conspiracy*, author Marilyn Ferguson refers to a network as a twentieth-century version of the ancient tribe and an instrument to attain the power to remake society. Moreover, because networking has an expansionist capacity, New Age leaders look upon it as a method for world unity and control. Networks are simple, unnoticed, and powerful. Furthermore, New Agers maintain that networks are synergistic, that is, they combine individual human energies into a collective force that can then be released to transform the world.

Although a low estimate of at least ten thousand different New Age organizations and groups network with one another in some fashion, the hub of much of the New Age networking exists in the form of several institutions and publications. While New Age networking is not necessarily hierarchical, several organizations do play a leading role.

One of these organizations is the Lucis Trust, formerly known as the Lucifer Publishing Company, a name far more revealing than its members now care to acknowledge. The parent organization for the Lucis Publishing Company and World Goodwill, the Lucis Trust translated and published the works of Theosophist Alice Bailey into many languages. The Lucis Trust, with an address in the United Nations Plaza, New York City, also supervises the Arcane School, which has trained thousands of graduates in the principles of theosophy and the New Age.

Also using a United Nations Plaza address is the organization known as Planetary Citizens, founded by United Nations Secretary General U Thant and Norman Cousins.[4] The board of directors of Planetary Citizens boasts some of the leadership of the New Age, including author-spokesperson David Spangler and Peter Caddy, founder of the New Age Findhorn Foundation in Scotland. Its stated goal is to support the World Servers who will prepare the world for the coming of "the Christ" and to "cross the threshold of consciousness" into a global view.

Closely linked with Planetary Citizens is the consortium known as the Planetary Initiative for the World We Choose which, in its networking of over three hundred New Age groups, represents a classic example of Aquarian linkage. Among its activities is the convening of a World Council of Wise Persons consisting of some influential intellectuals and artists involved in the New Age.

Another influential center of New Age networking is the Unity-in-Diversity Council, whose headquarters is located in Los Angeles. The very name suggests a syncretic concept found at the heart of Hinduism—that unity exists in diversity. On its board of directors can be found such New Age leaders as Peter Caddy, Robert Muller, and Swama Kriyanada. Its annual directory of members lists over two hundred New Age organizations, with an additional six hundred groups that maintain goals sympathetic to those of the Unity-in-Diversity Council. Among other activities, the Unity-in-Diversity Council publishes a newsletter, *Spectrum*, and sponsors New Age festivals.

Other publications such as magazines, newsletters, and books also serve to interconnect New Age followers. A *New Age Source Book*, *New Age Catalog*, and *New Age Directory* can now be purchased in leading bookstores in America. Magazines with such titles as *New Age Journal*, *New Age*, *Body Mind Spirit*, *New Realities*, and *Brain/Mind Bulle-*

tin have garnered a considerable circulation. New Age books seem to fare even better; whole sections in bookstores now may be labeled "New Age" or less specifically "Religion" or even "Inspirational." The casual browser may see Shirley MacLaine's *Out on a Limb* ironically sandwiched between the Chinese Taoist's *Tao Te Ching* and the Christian monk Thomas à Kempis' inspirational *Imitation of Christ*—such is the syncretic nature of New Age reading habits.

Another way New Age networking takes place is through special days of observance, festivals, conferences, and seminars. Several New Age observances have attracted worldwide attention. The Planetary Commission, under the leadership of New Age author John Randolph Price, sponsors an observance known as World Healing Day or Global Mind-Link.

On this day, to be held each year on December 31, all enlightened people of the world are to concentrate their collective energies in a gigantic, global meditation to usher in planetary healing and global peace. The Planetary Commission claims that on December 31, 1987, an estimated 875 million persons in eighty-two countries around the globe participated in World Healing Day. New Agers hope that such planetary observances will bring about an "empowerment" for a quantum leap into humanity's next evolutionary step.

Not only does the New Age Movement have its days of observance but it also sponsors festivals and fairs as a form of networking. The Unity-in-Diversity Council sponsors New World Festivals in major cities of the United States and Western Europe. These festivals or fairs each feature dozens of displays and exhibits which show off the wide potpourri of New Age activities Psy chics, channelers, and astrologers exhibit next to those who read crystals and balance energies. Book displays feature titles on self-healing, human potential, and yoga The fairs, which usually run for several days, attract informed New Agers as well as unsuspecting curiosity seekers.

But perhaps one of the most common forms of New Age networking is seminars held in a variety of forums as diverse as college campuses, business boardrooms, and church meeting halls. Topics vary from world peace to stress reduction. For example, World Goodwill of the Lucis Trust sponsored a seminar on Service to Humanity. Among the day's topics were global transformation and telepathic communication. The seminar ended with a "closing meditation."

Still other New Age seminars, some lasting several days to a week, tout such subjects as "Toward a Cosmic Community" or "Manifesting What You Want." These seminars often arouse further curiosity in participants, a curiosity which then leads to subsequent New Age involvement.

Thus the New Age Movement, which may appear at first to lack form, direction, or organization, does have goals, leadership, common spiritual experiences, and a multitiered system of networking. These give structure and objectives to the New Age Movement, even though the New Age involves many people who are quite unaware of such goals and plans. Nevertheless, the overall goal is expressly designed to bring mankind into the Age of Aquarius.

III

WHY IS IT SO INTRIGUING?

6
Subtle Deceptions

The search for a spiritual experience motivates people throughout the world, whatever their belief system might be. Because human beings are comprised of spirit as well as body, people from the most primitive to the most sophisticated societies seek to satisfy a spiritual urge. Within Western nations, this yearning for a greater meaning to life seems to increase when material desires are fulfilled.

In the search for spiritual understanding, many have turned to mysticism. As long ago as 1975, a national poll indicated that fully 40 percent of adult Americans believed they had had a genuine mystical experience. Given the rising interest in such experiences, we may assume that figure would be even higher today. In addition, unofficial estimates suggest that as much as 20 percent of the population of the United States and Western Europe has shifted its spiritual worldview to include Eastern religious influences.

For New Agers, a spiritual experience, sometimes called a "moment of enlightenment," represents the common denominator which ties together what might otherwise be quite divergent personalities and is a very important point in considering various aspects of the New Age. At a recent New Age fair, those present were asked why they had come. Although some said they were merely curious, most sought spiritual alternatives in order to deal with stress and tension. At the same time, they wanted to contribute somehow to a world of greater peace and harmony.

From a biblical viewpoint, however, the New Age spiritual experience must be labeled counterfeit. The danger of New Age spiritual and mystical experiences lies in their subtle and deceptive nature. For the unsuspecting, New Age spiritual terminology appears Christian in content, even when the experience leads far from true biblical Christianity.

Meditation

Perhaps the most common of New Age spiritual practices is meditation. All five of the world's great religions (Hinduism, Buddhism, Islam, Judaism, and Christianity) include meditation as a part of their teachings. The Bible, particularly the Old Testament, frequently refers to meditation. Beginning with Genesis, we read that Isaac went out into the field in the evening in order to meditate (Genesis 24:63).

When God spoke to Joshua following the death of Moses, He commanded, "Do not let this Book of the Law depart from your mouth; meditate on it day and night, so that you may be careful to do everything written in it.

Then you will be prosperous and successful" (Joshua 1:8).

This passage, as well as others in the Bible, clearly sets forth the difference between the Judeo-Christian concept of meditation and that of Hinduism and Buddhism, which has made its way into the New Age. Judeo-Christian meditation is designed to *fill* one's mind and spirit with the presence of God by meditating *upon* Him and His precepts.

The Psalmist makes this very clear in frequent references. In Psalm 1:2 we read, "But his delight is in the law of the Lord, and on his law he meditates day and night." Later the Psalmist writes, "I will meditate on all your works and consider all your mighty deeds" (Psalm 77:12). The longest of the Psalms, Psalm 119, contains frequent references to meditation on God's statutes, His precepts, and His words. Thus biblical meditation is encouraged for the purpose of seeking guidance, of acknowledging the awesome greatness of God and, above all, of basking in the wonderful presence of one's Creator.

Moreover, for the Christian, the motivation for meditation springs from a grateful heart that loves God and wants to please Him. Again, the Psalmist captures this spirit in Psalm 19:14: "May the words of my mouth and the meditation of my heart be pleasing in your sight, O Lord, my Rock and my Redeemer." The personal satisfaction of such meditation results from knowing that God is pleased with a voluntary human response inspired by love.

For the practitioner of Eastern meditation, however, the motivation and goal are much different. Here the meditator is encouraged not only to *empty* himself of all thoughts but also to concentrate on the divine *within* himself, the eternal "Thatness." The desire is to have a private, very personal experience rather than an experience that shows love to God.

Eastern meditation becomes a tool for seeking godlike status within oneself and for tapping into a "life force" which pervades all living things. Effort is directed inward to the small center of the self rather than upward to the loving and personal God of the universe. What could become a daily refreshing experience of self-renewal that comes from the worship and adoration of God instead becomes self-enthronement and a form of idolatry.

Several forms of Eastern meditation have gained popularity in the West, including Zen meditation, originating from Buddhist traditions. Zen meditation is often conducted in a special hall built for such purposes and is often practiced in the presence of numerous others under the direction of a Zen master. In Zen meditation, the meditator is first encouraged to empty his mind of all extraneous thoughts and then to center his thinking on a *koan*, or puzzle. Some *koans*, such as the following example, have gained notoriety even outside Zen circles: "If a tree falls down in the forest and no one is there to hear it, what happens to the sound?"

Of more popular acceptance has been Silva Mind Control, now referred to as the Silva Method. This form of meditation, begun by Jose Silva, has attracted an estimated 6 million devotees from over seventy countries. The program, taught over a period of thirty-two hours on two successive weekends, promises to the subscriber mental and spiritual powers to control circumstances as well as people by tapping into alpha levels of brain waves.

The best-known and most widespread form of Eastern

meditation practiced in the West is transcendental meditation, usually known as TM. From its Hindu origins, TM made its subtle way to the West via the Hindu guru Maharishi Mahesh Yogi, who gained world recognition after the Beatles spent time with him. After starting the Spiritual Regeneration Movement in England, the Maharishi discovered that the practice would be more acceptable in the United States, particularly in educational circles, if it were cloaked in scientific terms. Thus the name Science of Creative Intelligence was adopted and the American Foundation for the Science of Creative Intelligence established to bring TM discipline into the business community. The Maharishi International University was opened in Fairfield, Iowa, with additional plans to establish thirty-six hundred training centers all over the world.

A sample of what TM promises can be seen in an advertisement run in the September 17, 1987, edition of the *Colorado Daily*, campus newspaper of the University of Colorado. Bold headlines state, "If you really want to know how to improve your grades, your career, and your life, there's an upcoming lecture you shouldn't miss." The full-page ad announces that over 1 million students have reduced stress, increased intelligence, decreased drug and alcohol abuse, and even improved athletic performance through the practice of fifteen to twenty minutes per day of the TM technique. The ad states that scientific research has proven the success of TM. It challenges students to make a contribution to world peace by practicing TM and to help lead the world into a more orderly and progressive state.

Such advertising suggests a social and scientific veneer for a concept that is not only spiritual but also very Hindu in its origins. The Maharishi has said that the major problem with every human being is the failure to tap into his own divine being and thus enter into cosmic consciousness and god-consciousness, the motivation that forms the foundation of Hinduism. He encourages his followers to merge their individuality into pure "Being," to concentrate on the "Eternal Thatness." Only then can human beings realize their full potential and thus achieve a major goal of the New Age, also known as the Human Potential Movement.

What has also attracted followers to the Maharishi's conveniently altered brand of Hinduism is that he does not condemn materialism. Whereas Hindu mystics in India may renounce all material possessions and wander into the Himalayas wearing only a loincloth, the Maharishi's Western devotees may pursue happiness materially as well as spiritually.

To date, some 8 million persons in the United States have taken the steps of initiation to enter the practice of transcendental meditation. After an introductory lecture, interested persons are wooed back to pay a sizable sum and thus receive their mantra. A mantra consists of a Sanskrit syllable or sound to be repeated over and over in meditation, a practice as old as Hinduism itself. Follow-up sessions check the initiate's progress until eventually he is encouraged to take "advanced courses" offered at training centers.

Alarmingly, TM has been allowed to enter the nation's public schools and prison system under the guise of a scientific method intended to reduce stress and bring about harmony. Sadly, many Christians have been misled into believing that somehow TM, Hindu in its origins, can enrich the Christian experience and was actually taught by Jesus and His disciples. Such a deception has no biblical foundation whatsoever.

Not only are TM and other forms of Eastern meditation subtle deceptions but they have also proven to be dangerous to the mental, emotional, and spiritual stability of their adherents. First, those who take up forms of meditation are often hurting, desperate persons looking for life's answers. Thus they enter the meditative experience in an emotionally and spiritually vulnerable state that clouds the deceptive nature of the practice. The enticing promises give a false hope to vulnerable persons that they at last have found the answers to their problems.

Perhaps it is an attestation to the dangers of Eastern spiritual experiences that a Spiritual Emergency Network has been set up on the campus of the California Institute of Transpersonal Psychology in San Francisco as a treatment center for "transpersonal emergencies." This term is a euphemism for those numerous victims who suffer serious mental and physical reactions during spiritual experiences, including Eastern meditation. The network, and an additional forty-two similar regional centers, was established by New Agers Christina and Stanislav Grof. Although the Grofs refer to their clients as being in difficult stages of spiritual growth, former devotees of TM and other forms of Eastern meditation testify to frightening and bizarre experiences that affect their psychological and physical well-being. How glaringly such stories stand in contrast to the peaceful and fulfilling effects of Christian meditation such as that described by the Psalmist.

Despite these dangers and warnings, meditation is now accepted in mainstream America. If a visitor were in Washington, D.C., on a Friday, he could find a group meditating at the Pentagon. These decision makers call themselves the Spiritual Defense Initiative as they meditate for world peace.

Prestigious medical institutions such as The Johns Hopkins Hospital now prescribe meditation as a means of treating medical problems. What was once identified with the gurus and hippies of the 1960s has now been adopted as "scientific" in the 1990s.

Yoga

Ask any Hindu living in a village in India and he will tell you that yoga is a very integral part of his ancient religion. Today Westerners have embraced yoga wholeheartedly. Millions of people regularly practice yoga from their living room floors in front of TV sets, beside their swimming pools, in college classrooms, or at the nearest YMCA. If one were to confront a Westerner practicing his yoga positions with the fact that he is actually conducting a Hindu exercise, he might be incredulous or even outraged. Those who market yoga have convinced their Western audience that yoga exercises are purely physical and can be divorced from the spiritual. Those who truly understand yoga know better.

What is yoga? The word itself comes from the same root as the word *yoke* in English. In ancient Sanskrit, *yoga* means "to unite" as well as "to place under discipline." The intent is integration—in this case, the integration of the spirit and body with the ultimate goal of reaching a state of detachment, known in the West as an "altered state of consciousness."

When we trace the origins of yoga, our search takes us to the ancient Hindu sacred texts, specifically to the *Bhagavad Gita*, in which the Hindu hero god, Lord Krishna, introduces yoga as a pathway to heaven. Shiva, the Destroyer, one of Hinduism's leading deities within its elaborate pantheon of gods and goddesses, is also depicted as the Lord of Yoga. In this way the connection is made between yoga and its potentially destructive powers

In Hinduism, yoga represents the pathway to oneness with the Absolute (Brahman) and is the multifaceted discipline chosen by most Hindus. Many forms of Yoga exist within Hinduism, including *jnana yoga, bhakti yoga, raja yoga, karma yoga*, and *hatha yoga*, which is one of the most advanced forms and has attracted considerable interest in the West.

But what Westerners do not seem to understand, as they naively enter into yoga disciplines, is that the intent of the Hindu yogis in developing yogic techniques was not to produce better physiques or to tone muscles but to enter into an advanced spiritual state. Even Richard Hittleman, whose books on yoga have gained wide circulation in the United States, admits that yoga is not primarily a series of physical exercises designed for health purposes.

In fact, those who know the power behind yoga as well as the intent of it acknowledge that the practice can be both dangerous and destructive for the unprepared. Even in India, devotees of yoga are not permitted to practice the advanced *hatha yoga* (now promoted in the West) unless they have first mastered certain prerequisites involving the mind and body. Most persons practicing yoga go through a series of exercises known as *asanas* and learn a deep-breathing technique known as *pranayama*. These routines are designed to tap the vital energy source and entice one to move deeper into the yogic experience, which ultimately becomes a flirtation with destruction.

Of considerable danger to the yogic practitioner is the awakening of what yogis refer to as *Kundalini.* To a Hindu, Kundalini is a serpent goddess who resides at the base of the human spine and who, when aroused, can exert tremendous power in and through the human being. Seven *chakras* or energy centers lodge along the spine and, when worked through by advanced yogis in a series of special exercises, arouse Kundalini. But even in India the arousal of Kundalini has been known to produce bizarre and permanently debilitating results, including great physical pain, manic-depression, and insanity. Many of those unfortunate Western victims who have ended up in treatment centers as the "transpersonal emergencies" mentioned in the previous section represent the dark side of yoga.

Nevertheless, despite its Hindu nature and its acknowledged dangers, yoga is openly advertised and promoted on TV, in catalogs, newspapers, and on college campuses. Often yoga comes packaged as a health-and-exercise routine or as a spiritual answer to stress and tension. The Integral Yoga Headquarters in Virginia touts yoga as an ecumenical discipline which enhances the spiritual life of followers of all religions. Interestingly, the Virginia headquarters houses shrines to all major and lesser religions as well as a shrine to the "unknown religion." A major figure of the Integral Yoga Headquarters, Swami Satchidananda, directs yoga seminars throughout the Western world, including the Soviet Union, speaking on such subtle themes as "World Peace Begins With You."

Not only has yoga given birth to a seminar and retreat business but it has also been packaged in videocassette form by one of America's leading yoga teachers. Prospective buyers are promised opportunities to "stretch, strengthen, and relax at home . . . relax, relieve stress, and increase vitality." The second volume promises a "deeper experience." For those desiring a different product, a yoga video includes "humor . . . state-of-the-art special effects, and contemporary music" to produce an enjoyable yogic experience. But whether it is practiced under a tree outside an Indian village or via a cassette tape beside a swimming pool, yoga is yoga.

Reincarnation

Just as a spiritual experience represents the common denominator which ties together millions of New Age followers, a belief in reincarnation threads its way through almost all New Age philosophy and has become an integral part of the New Age worldview. Polls have suggested that almost one-fourth of the population of the Western world believes in reincarnation.

By definition, those who believe in reincarnation suggest that a soul begins its journey in the universe as a one-celled organism or perhaps a mineral, then wends its way upward through plant and animal status until at last the soul reaches the status of a human being. Having reached such a station, the soul will then be reincarnated into subsequent human beings until it reaches liberation, a state known in Hinduism as *moksha* or *samadhi* and in Buddhism as *nirvana*. That state represents oneness with Brahman, the Absolute, the Divine.

The belief in reincarnation can be traced back thousands of years, possibly as early as the Babylonian Mystery Religion referred to in chapter 3. Certainly reincarnation comprises a major theme in the religions of Hinduism and Buddhism.

According to reincarnationists, the vehicle which propels the soul along its reincarnational journey is the Law of Karma, sometimes referred to as the "universal law of cause and effect." The Law of Karma postulates that whatever circumstance a human finds himself in in his present life is due to the behavior and moral decisions made in a past human life. Moreover, moral behavior of this life predetermines the karma which the present human soul carries into the next incarnation. In India, reincarnation, with its partner, the Law of Karma, forms the basis of the caste system. Whatever caste one is born into results from the karma passed on from a previous human lifetime.

Thus both good and bad karma are passed on in the universe. Because each soul moves on to a new human body and assumes a new personality, a human takes on the karma from some previous person. For example, the bad karma built up by a mass murderer may be passed on to a little girl who might be born handicapped. The human personality of the murderer has ceased to exist but his bad karma has now entered another human being, in this case, an unfortunate child who had no control over the circumstances of her birth. Thus bad karma can never really be done away with but merely goes on to new human forms.

From a Christian viewpoint, reincarnation not only has no biblical basis whatsoever, but it also cannot explain the questions of justice and mercy or of good and evil. Whereas the reincarnationists' view of the universe is an impersonal one, the Christian viewpoint states that the universe is ruled by a sovereign, infinite, but *personal* God. Furthermore, the existence of evil in the world is biblically explained as the result of man's fallen condition, which has severed his fellowship with a holy God—a condition called sin.

Although the God of the Bible is a God of justice, because of the nature of His character, He is also a God of mercy. Because of who He is, He cannot act otherwise. While He has every right to mete out justice for man's evil acts, yet His great, eternal act of mercy was shown when, at Calvary, the iniquities of all mankind were placed upon the crucified Jesus. Since that time, salvation for each human being is a gift waiting to be accepted. Paul writes in Ephesians 2:8, 9, "For it is by grace you have been saved, through faith—and this not from yourselves, it is the gift of God—not by works, so that no one can boast." Thus, mankind's future was forever altered by divine mercy.

For the reincarnationist, however, the question of evil and suffering in the world can never be resolved. Karma provides no mercy, no forgiveness, and no hope. Furthermore, such a belief system eliminates true human compassion toward the suffering. Jesus encouraged acts of compassion toward the less fortunate when He said, "I tell you the truth, whatever you did for one of the least of these brothers of mine, you did for me" (Matthew 25:40). Whereas the Hindu Brahman (high caste member) may walk down a street in Calcutta and ignore a suffering leper lying on the sidewalk as a victim of bad karma, the Christian Missionaries of Charity reach out in the compassion motivated by the words and deeds of Jesus.

Western reincarnationists have sometimes argued that

the Bible teaches reincarnation. For example, they cite the words of Jesus to Nicodemus: "I tell you the truth, no one can see the kingdom of God unless he is born again" (John 3:3). Nicodemus was mystified, concluding that Jesus meant physical rebirth. However, Jesus went on to clarify the statement and, in so doing, struck down the reincarnationists' argument. Jesus responded, "I tell you the truth, no one can enter the kingdom of God unless he is born of water and the Spirit. Flesh gives birth to flesh, but the Spirit gives birth to spirit" (John 3:5, 6). Thus Jesus was not referring to physical birth and rebirth; He clearly meant a spiritual rebirth. The Bible also refutes reincarnation in Hebrews 9:27: "Man is destined to die once, and after that to face judgment."

Resurrection represents the biblical term for what takes place after death. The mortal body dies but takes on an immortal body which will never die again. Such resurrection means each human soul is distinctive, with a unique personality that will not be passed on to some other human. In fact, Paul places the doctrine of resurrection at the heart of Christianity when he writes, "If there is no resurrection of the dead, then not even Christ has been raised. And if Christ has not been raised, our preaching is useless and so is your faith" (1 Corinthians 15:13, 14).

Furthermore, reincarnationists sometimes argue that past-life recall offers proof of reincarnation. A celebrated example of past-life recall was the 1950s story of Bridey Murphy, in which a Colorado housewife named Ruth Simmons claimed, under hypnosis, that she had once been an Irish girl named Bridey Murphy. Although her facts seemed to check out with the real existence of such a girl, the case proved to be a hoax when it was revealed that

Simmons' subconscious mind retained many facts passed on to her from the Irish nanny of her own childhood.

Likewise, most other cases of past-life recall either have proven to be hoaxes or can be explained by natural experiences or by the phenomenon known as cryptoamnesia. Cryptoamnesia occurs when the human mind, under an altered state of consciousness such as hypnosis, recalls facts and perceptions stored in the phenomenal human memory bank. It should be noted here that, despite considerable research, hypnosis remains a little-understood activity. Finally, past-life recall can be attributed to contact with spirit beings, a subject to be treated in another chapter.

Reincarnation has appeal among Westerners, including many well-educated persons, because such a belief provides an escape from the gnawing issue of sin in one's own life. To believe that there will be repeated opportunities to somehow achieve personal salvation relieves the need to eliminate certain immoral behavioral patterns in one's present life. One can only hope that good karma will counterbalance the bad. The tragedy in such a belief lies in the rejection of the gift of personal salvation provided for every human who accepts that gift, lovingly given by the death of Jesus on Calvary.

Thus New Agers attempt to satisfy their personal search for spiritual fulfillment through meditation, yoga, and a belief in reincarnation. Another theme weaving its way through the New Age Movement is the occult. To that broad but pertinent and controversial topic we now turn.

7
Occult New Age

Not too long ago, *occult* was a word whispered in private. If someone dabbled in the occult, that person's activities were spoken of in hushed tones and may well have been an embarrassment to family and friends. But today, the occult is in vogue. Movies and TV programs openly flaunt themes of the occult; during interviews, movie stars eagerly discuss personal occult experiences; rock musicians choose occult titles for their songs and refer to the occult in their lyrics; major bookstores feature entire sections labeled simply "Occult" or, with more subtlety, "Religion and Philosophy."

What has happened to alter the public's perception of the occult? Perhaps the most significant change of the last decade is that matters of the occult are now regarded as scientific and thus acceptable and respectable, even if still unexplainable.

What is the occult? Its Latin root means "to cover up or hide." Dictionaries define *occult* as that which is beyond understanding, mysterious, and unexplainable, pertaining to magic, divination, and incantation. Today, in a broad sense, the occult includes those occurrences which are outside of normal spiritual practice and which are phenomenal in nature even if unexplainable in appearance. A list of occult activities would include, among other practices, astrology, channeling, tarot cards, clairvoyance, Ouija boards, astral projection, crystal consciousness, fortune-telling, palmistry, numerology, and black magic.

The argument as to whether art imitates life or life imitates art remains an ongoing debate. In the case of the occult, it is difficult to discern whether movies, TV, music, and publications are pandering to what the public demands or whether they are vehicles to fashion public thinking. Perhaps the truth lies in both arguments. Whatever the case, irrefutably, Western society currently shows an enormously increased interest in the occult. A University of Chicago poll indicated that some 67 percent of the public claims to have had psychic experiences.[1] Bookstores find that titles dealing with the occult are among the fastest selling and most sought after of any current literary category.

Interestingly, the prestigious Literary Guild includes a section labeled "New Age" in its catalog. The Winter 1989 edition included in its New Age category books on numerology, fortune-telling by use of tarot cards, and sets of karma cards—all occult topics. Likewise, Time-Life Books, with a distinguished record of credible publications, recently embarked on an extensive advertising campaign for its series "Mysteries of the Unknown." This series offers such tantalizing but occult topics as *Psychic Powers, Psychic Voyages,* and *Phantom Encounters.* These discuss out-of-body experiences, reincarnation, astral projection, and psychic healing.

Significantly, the occult and the New Age Movement are inseparably linked. Beyond the goal of ushering in a new age by leading mankind to one world government and one world religion ruled by one leader rests the New Age common denominator: a mystical spiritual experience. For most New Agers, this mystical experience, this "moment of enlightenment," falls within the category of the occult. For millions of others who perhaps would never identify themselves as part of the New Age Movement, a flirtation with the Ouija board or astrology or ESP has enticed them into an occult experience. Unfortunately, in the case of the occult, the wonderfully innate gift of human curiosity opens a destructive Pandora's box which leads deeper and deeper into an abyss of darkness.

The Bible very clearly prohibits any participation in occult activities. One of the strongest biblical warnings against the occult can be found in Deuteronomy 18:10–13, where occult practices are labeled "detestable." In this passage, the people of Israel are warned:

> Let no one be found among you who sacrifices his son or daughter in the fire, who practices divination or sorcery, interprets omens, engages in witchcraft, or casts spells, or who is a medium or spiritist or who consults the dead. Anyone who does these things is detestable to the Lord, and because of these detestable practices the Lord your God will drive out those nations before you. You must be blameless before the Lord your God.

Because of the unchangeable nature of God and His laws, this warning is as applicable today as it was when it was first given.

Channeling

"Why is Lazaris so special? Why is he unique? . . . He is a friend who helps us grow by showing us the blockages and limitations we put in our own path. Then he lovingly shows us how to remove the obstacles with a variety of techniques. . . ." This pronouncement in an ad in a Hawaiian newspaper is part of an occult activity called "channeling," which now attracts a following in virtually every part of the United States. Lazaris is a medium who "channels" through a former Florida insurance salesman named Jach Pursel. The announcement also says, ". . . Lazaris, a non-physical entity who channels through Jach Pursel, beautifully combines practical technique with Spiritual [sic] insights."[2] Pursel collects more than a million dollars per year on his seminars, videocassettes, and counseling. Channeling has become big business.

What is channeling? It is simply the modern name for consulting with a medium or seeking the advice of a spirit entity, a practice that is absolutely condemned in the Bible. Not only does the Deuteronomy passage cited earlier warn against mediumship but other references do as well. Leviticus 19:31 exhorts, "Do not turn to mediums or seek out spiritists, for you will be defiled by them. I am the Lord your God." Despite this biblical condemnation, channeling has attracted a large following.

One of the best-known channelers of recent years has been J. Z. Knight, a former housewife, who channels the voice of "Ramtha," who claims to have lived on earth some thirty-five thousand years ago. Today, in a husky voice, Ramtha gives advice to thousands who flock to seminars, paying from four hundred dollars to fifteen hundred dollars in their search for spiritual answers. Ramtha's message is the same as that of the Tempter in the Garden of Eden: You are your own god; there is neither right nor wrong, good nor evil, and, best of all, no such thing as sin.[3]

Ramtha goes on to advise that people should move out of big cities into the northwestern part of the United States which, according to Ramtha, represents the safest area in which to live. Incredibly, hundreds of Americans have pulled up stakes, sold all they had, and migrated to rural areas of Washington, Idaho, Oregon, Montana, and northern California—all on the advice of a thirty-five-thousand-year-old-spirit!

But Jach Pursel and J. Z. Knight are not exclusive in their channeling. Now New Agers by the hundreds are getting their own "spirit guides." Shirley MacLaine makes no secret of her channeling with a spirit guide. Penny Torres, a Los Angeles police officer's wife, channels an entity called Mafu. A spirit entity called Seth regularly channels through several persons since the death of his best-known channeler, Jane Roberts.

Now, "how-to" seminars are being offered to teach anyone to channel. Why pay fifteen hundred dollars to someone else when you can have your own spirit guide? In a popular Colorado New Age newspaper, an advertisement announces, "Channeling is a skill! We provide you with supportive preparation and follow-up exercises designed to take you step by step to becoming more aware of non-physical energy, until you are able to connect with your own Guide's energy." The ad then announces three weekend training seminars.[4]

Not surprisingly, the *glasnost* policy of the Soviet Union has not only opened the nation to a flow of Western goods and ideas but also to New Age influence. On its nightly news, NBC featured a segment showing a Soviet citizen who channels before a live audience on a nationally televised broadcast that is eagerly watched by millions of Russians. The same NBC report showed a Russian psychic healer who claims to send his healing power across the airwaves through the subtle movements of his hands.

Interestingly, whatever form the spirit guides take or through whomever they channel, their message is the same: You are your own god and can create your own reality. The Big Lie of Genesis 3 has never disappeared. If there are thousands of spirit guides available and their message is the same, who are they and where do they come from? As will be discussed more fully in the next chapter, these spirit guides are part of that huge array of fallen angels, now become demons, who accompanied Lucifer when he was expelled from heaven in a great rebellious upheaval. These spirit guides form part of that power of spiritual darkness against whom the Apostle Paul warned in Ephesians 6:11, 12.

Crystal Consciousness

Another trendy New Age activity which employs occult power is "crystal consciousness," the belief that rock crystals radiate a form of spiritual energy. Ancient religions often ascribed spiritual powers to certain rocks and gemstones, and today that belief is being revived. Such stones as quartz crystal, amethyst, topaz, tourmaline, and citrine are used for psychic healing, to clear the air of negative vibrations, and to create positive thinking.

Not surprisingly, crystal consciousness has become big business along with channeling and other New Age activities. First, of course, are the shops that sell crystals in every shape and form. Some of the crystals remain in their natural state, both large and small, while others are carved into beautiful designs or made into jewelry. The best crystals are not cheap, however. A crystal shop in New York's glitzy Trump Tower recently offered a huge crystal for the price of $360,000.

But the simple purchase of a crystal is only the first step along the path to crystal consciousness. After careful selection, the stone must then be cleansed, a process that can be done at home or by a "professional." Cleansing a crystal is carried out either in ocean water or salt water, followed by exposing the rock to both the sun and the moon for at least twenty-four hours. For ultimate effectiveness of the crystal, however, it must then be programmed to respond to certain situations. Crystal programming is offered in the form of forty-five-dollar seminars or twenty-four dollar videocassette kits. Sometimes the purchase price of a crystal includes cleansing and programming.

If, for example, the crystal is to be used to produce positive thinking, it must be programmed for this purpose. Other crystals are programmed to produce good dreams when placed under the pillow, while still others are programmed to reduce jet lag, to calm pets, or even to reduce hangovers. Some people have taken to drinking "crystal cocktails," tonic water in which crystals have been dropped to produce a desired result.

But perhaps one of the most common uses of crystal power is its psychic healing. This practice, based upon a Hindu concept of power centers located along the human spine known as *chakras*, involves placing the crystals over the seven *chakra* points. The crystals, which have been previously programmed for healing, then channel health into those *chakra* points of the body to affect vital organs.

Not only is crystal consciousness a popular New Age practice in the United States but it now attracts devotees worldwide as well. In 1988, a "Crystal Link" from Los Angeles to Moscow hooked up crystal lovers via audiovisual link for an exchange of "peace and friendship." *Vogue* magazine, the handbook of current fashion trends both in the United States and Europe, recently featured a five-page article on crystal consciousness in which crystals were touted as ". . . a small piece of the cosmos you can carry in your pocket . . ." (August 1988). The article not only described the attributes of crystal consciousness but also listed the many celebrities who are involved in this occult activity.

From a biblical viewpoint, not only is channeling through the use of crystals another example of mediumship but crystal consciousness also represents an example of what Paul refers to in Romans 1:25. In this passage, the apostle warns against those who worship created things rather than the Creator. He writes, "They exchanged the truth of God for a lie, and worshiped and served created things rather than the Creator—who is forever praised. Amen." What the Bible warns against has now found a trendy home across the nation from New York's posh Fifth Avenue to Beverly Hills' opulent Rodeo Drive.

Astrology

In 1988, Americans were surprised to learn of the reported influence of astrology in the White House, where some scheduling decisions may have been based upon astrologers' advice. They needn't have reacted with such surprise: millions of Americans dabble in astrology every day. Surveys suggest that as many as 30 million Americans believe in astrology and that some 77 percent of adults can readily identify their astrological sign. Some 2,000 newspapers feature astrological advice and horoscopes on a daily basis (sometimes running the same horoscopes year after year) while fully 175,000 part-time and 10,000 full-time astrologers practice this ancient form of the occult.[5]

The belief that the position of heavenly bodies somehow influences human affairs dates back long before the time of Christ, particularly to the era of ancient Babylon. Perhaps as early as 2,000 B.C. astrologers had identified five planets and ascribed mystical powers to the heavenly bodies. A zodiac may have been drawn up by the ancient Egyptians, used by the Babylonians, and later transmitted to Greece and India sometime in the fourth century B.C.

However, natal astrology, the belief that the moment of one's birth places a person under an astrological sign, dates back to the Greek astronomer Ptolemy (A.D. 127–151). It was he who first assigned births to the twelve signs of the zodiac, which are still used by astrologers today. Ironically, Ptolemy's calculations were wrong because he subscribed to a geocentric view of the universe, which placed the earth, rather than the sun, at the center of the universe. Furthermore, because of the way the earth "wobbles" on its axis, the zodiac Ptolemy designed has now moved one entire astrological house backward. Moreover, any horoscope based upon the Ptolemaic signs of the zodiac are incorrect because all of the planets had not yet been discovered in Ptolemy's day. Yet natal astrology continues to attract a worldwide following.

Interest in astrology ranges from those who casually glance at their horoscope predictions in the newspaper each morning to those who base their life decisions upon astrology. Somewhere in between is a large group of persons who read books on astrology, who ask, "What is your sign?" and who judge personality types based upon astrological signs. Those who take astrology very seriously willingly pay large sums to astrologers who claim to have psychic gifts to foretell the future. A surprising number of influential business decisions are made only after consultation with astrologers.

The latest twist in the astrology business is what might be called "New Age astrology" in which certain psychic vibrations are ascribed to the universe. The astrologer then taps into these universal energy vibrations to produce an individualized horoscope processed through computer technology. This form of universal vibration astrology goes a step further by viewing the planets as deities with certain qualities based upon the Roman gods and goddesses for whom the planets were named. For example, Mars is thought of as the "god of war," Venus as the "goddess of love," and so forth. Astrological decisions are then based upon these character attributes as well as on their planetary position in the universe.

The Bible condemns the practice of astrology. In the Old Testament, Deuteronomy's list of detestable practices includes the interpretation of omens (Deuteronomy 18:10). Later, we find that one of the reasons God punished Israel was for the sin of idolatry. Among their idolatrous practices was worshiping the "starry hosts" of their pagan neighbors (2 Kings 17:16). The Prophet Isaiah challenged the stargazers and astrologers of Babylon to save the nation. Referring to the inadequacy of the astrologers of the day, he wrote, "Surely they are like stubble; the fire will burn them up. They cannot even save themselves from the power of the flame" (Isaiah 47:14).

It is perhaps an irony of New Age thinking that many New Agers, while subscribing to the major New Age principle of the "divine within," that each person is his own god, also follow the ancient occult practice of astrology, in which it is believed that one's destiny is controlled by the heavenly bodies. Nevertheless, the central principle of the New Age, which suggests that an Age of Aquarius is dawning, ties the New Age Movement into astrology. In order to make astrology more acceptable, some have labeled it a science or pseudoscience. The fact remains, however, that from a biblical perspective, astrology is a form of the occult and is therefore unacceptable to God.

The Supernatural

Part of what makes the occult so intriguing to many people is its unexplainable and mysterious quality. Much about the occult lies within the realm of the supernatural: that which cannot be explained by natural laws and which is beyond normal human capability. The Bible contains numerous examples of the supernatural, beginning with the plagues Moses brought down upon Egypt and continuing with the miracles performed by Jesus.

However, in the New Testament Paul warns Corinth, a city that had more than a passing interest in the occult. The apostle writes in 2 Corinthians 11:14, "Satan himself masquerades as an angel of light." Part of the subtlety of the New Age Movement lies in its counterfeit spiritual experiences. These are occurrences which seem very close to biblical accounts but are in fact counterfeits which do not glorify Jesus Christ. Such supernatural phenomena include clairvoyance, the alleged power to see objects or persons from beyond the natural limits of eyesight. Another is extrasensory perception (ESP) or the capacity to communicate or perceive beyond natural sensory distances.

One of the most deceptive offerings within this category of the supernatural is a packaged set of books called *A Course in Miracles.* This three-volume work has now sold over two hundred thousand copies and is also available in an attractive package of forty-two audiotape cassettes. Presently translated into twenty languages, this deceptive course was first published in 1976 by the Foundation for Inner Peace. Its statement of purpose suggests that blocks to awareness may serve as a detriment to love's presence and can be miraculously removed. Among the tenets of *A Course in Miracles* are the following: There are no sins, only mistakes; an individual can program his mind to replace fear with love; the Son of God is not Jesus but our collective Christ-consciousness.

While the vocabulary of *A Course in Miracles* sounds Christian, this popular New Age series represents an occult-based example of the way darkness masquerades as light The author of *A Course in Miracles* was the late Helen Schucman, a psychology professor at Columbia University. By her own admission, the course was channeled to her through the medium of automatic writing over a period of seven years. Sadly, *A Course in Miracles* is offered in Christian churches and numerous seminars throughout the United States.

Not only does *A Course in Miracles* represent a very subtle deception but it also serves as a reminder of the importance of what the beloved disciple John wrote in the first century A.D. In 1 John 4:1–3 we read:

> Dear friends, do not believe every spirit, but test the spirits to see whether they are from God, because many false prophets have gone out into the world. This is how you can recognize the Spirit of God: Every spirit that acknowledges that Jesus Christ has come in the flesh is from God, but every spirit that does not acknowledge Jesus is not from God.

Based upon these qualifications, *A Course in Miracles* fails the test of Christian authenticity.

Unquestionably, the New Age Movement includes much that lies within the realm of the occult. Many who are deeply involved in the occult know precisely the nature of their practices, the source of their powers, and the Prince of Darkness with whom they are dealing. However, millions of others are naively involved in some aspect of occult New Age without realizing that such practices are strictly forbidden in the Bible.

Unfortunately, the nature of the occult is such that a little easily grows into larger proportions. Humans are characteristically very curious beings. In the case of the occult, that same curiosity which leads to a seemingly innocent flirtation with the occult soon leads to a courtship and finally a marriage with the occult in which the curious seeker has been drawn into a quagmire of spiritual darkness.

A host of diverse New Age activities seem to offer something for everyone. For the physically ill, there is holistic health; for the businessman, there are self-actualization seminars; for educators, there is a whole alternative curriculum; for children, there are cartoons, games, movies, and books. In the next section, we will find out why these activities are gradually making their way into almost every area of Western life.

IV

WHY DO PEOPLE GET INVOLVED?

8
Holistic Health Care

The maintenance of good health and health care are of interest to everyone. In the United States, the health-care industry has become a billion-dollar enterprise as skyrocketing costs for treatment of the sick reach alarming proportions. Such high costs for professional health care, coupled with a sense of disillusionment over medical techniques, have driven many persons to seek alternative means of healing. Increasingly, Westerners are turning to holistic health care and its more traditional and even ancient practices.

The term *holistic* is derived from the Greek word *holos*, meaning "whole." Hence, the goal of holistic health care is to produce a healthy person in mind, body, and spirit. Few persons, including Christians, would disagree with the need for humans to be healthy in every area of their being. Because we are spirit as well as body, not only is a healthy spirit necessary but it often represents the key to a healthy body.

However, the area of holistic health care is an arena of Western culture in which the "buyer must beware." Not only can holistic health care be very expensive but it doesn't guarantee its promises. Even beyond these considerations, many aspects of holistic health inculcate and integrate New Age philosophy. Although it would be a mistake to label all forms of traditional and holistic health care as part of the New Age, caution must be exercised in accepting holistic techniques.

The Holistic Approach

Perhaps one of the best ways to understand the subject is to consider certain basic presuppositions upon which the holistic approach is based. First is the belief that humans are body, mind, and spirit and that all three must be treated in order to achieve full health. Second is the belief that humans can control their own health because they have *within them* the resources to ward off illness and destroy disease. Closely related to this presupposition is the belief that because humans can control their own health, there is a potential for mankind to become healthier and more perfect in a gradual evolutionary process.

The third presupposition suggests that scientific, established medical procedures are dehumanizing and mechanistic while the methods fail to treat the entire person. Prescription drugs and surgical techniques are viewed as unnecessary and expensive treatments which are actually detrimental to restoration of good health.

The alternative, holistic health practitioners suggest, is a return to traditional, age-old methods, including use of a wide range of herbs, plant derivatives, dietary changes, meditative techniques, and changes of life-style. Such suggestions represent a fourth presupposition of the holistic movement. A fifth principle views death as a part of the physical and spiritual evolutionary process and is even seen by some as a nonexistent state and an illusion. Here we can see the influence of the belief in reincarnation discussed in a previous chapter. This Hindu-based belief suggests that humans simply continue on and on in an endless cycle of birth and rebirth until at last they are released into oneness with the universal Energy Force.

Proceed With Caution

Much of what falls within the broad category of holistic health care seems attractive, appropriate, and makes good sense, particularly in the face of questions concerning costs and techniques of modern medical care. Why, then, must caution be exercised?

First, we must consider the underlying explanation for several of the holistic presuppositions. What is the premise behind the suggestion that each person can control his own health? At the basis of this presupposition rests one of the main themes which ties the New Age together: Each person possesses the "divine within." Again we see the appearance of the "Big Lie" of Genesis 3: Humans can be like God.

This argument posits that "if I am godlike, I ought to have within me the powers not only to heal myself but also to maintain good health." The "divine within" principle compels the person toward self-realization and self-actualization which, when taken to their ultimate end, produce self-enthronement. Self-enthronement represents a form of idolatry which is antibiblical.

Unfortunately, this presupposition that each person has within him the power to heal himself is a formula for disappointment and further disillusionment. Persons seeking holistic health care often are seriously ill and may have exhausted modern medical techniques. At such times, patients are both vulnerable and desperate. If, by seeking a release of their internal resources via meditation or visualization techniques, they are unable to heal themselves, such unfortunate patients become victims of self-induced guilt and a sense of inadequacy and personal failure. Their physical illness has now been complicated by emotional and spiritual trauma.

A second major reason for the unsuspecting to exercise caution when considering holistic health care can be found in the motivation, origins, and methodology of holistic treatments. Is the motivation to activate an "energy force," or perhaps the *ki* (Chinese term), or *prana* (Hindu term), and thus unite with the Energy Force of the universe? The use of such terminology should serve as a cautionary red light and cause the patient to ask more questions about the practitioner's belief system.

Furthermore, the patient who considers holistic health care would do well to investigate the origins of techniques which are to be used. While the goal of integration of body, mind, and spirit is a lofty aspiration against which little argument exists, the suggested pathway to such wholeness may find its origins in Eastern religions, mystical traditions, shamanism, or even the occult.

For example, one ancient medical technique now often found within holistic circles is acupuncture. This traditional Chinese method dates back at least five thousand years and bases its healing principle upon the Taoist concept of *yin and yang* (*see* chapter 3). According to this principle, in order to maintain good health, the perfect balance of complementary but opposing forces must be maintained. This balance can be brought about by inserting specially designed needles into some of over one thousand acupuncture points on the human body. These points are located along fourteen meridians in the body, which in turn connect organs and cause an energy flow (*ki*) to move unimpeded.

Acupressure is based upon the same principles but excludes the use of needles. Despite the millennia of acupuncture use, medical doctors in the West still doubt the beneficial therapeutic results of acupuncture.

Closely related to acupuncture in its principles is the holistic technique known as biofeedback. This therapy makes use of the patient's own mind to gain control of otherwise involuntary states. The patient's state of mind is monitored by electrical devices in order to reveal undesirable responses and thus alter his thought patterns. Biofeedback is sometimes used to treat such maladies as muscle aches, headaches, and high blood pressure.

Certainly the long-term results of biofeedback are still questioned by the medical profession, Christian or non-Christian. From a Christian perspective, the origins of biofeedback must also be examined. The root of biofeedback lies in Eastern mysticism. The same principle of mind over matter which allows a Hindu yogi to stand on one leg for a year or to sit unclothed in a Himalayan snowbank also governs biofeedback. Furthermore, patients utilizing biofeedback techniques often report experiences of altered states of consciousness or of deep meditation leading to depression.

A glance through a newspaper that advertises holistic health care reveals the variety of techniques encompassed by this broad category: Chiropractic (therapy through manipulation of the spine); osteopathy (manipulation of other parts of the body as well as the spine); homeopathy (use of small doses of a remedy which in large doses produces the effects of the disease being treated); foot reflexology (application of pressure to points on the foot to relieve pain elsewhere in the body); myotherapy (use of pressure and stretching to relieve pain); aromatherapy (use of aromatic essences to provide care and comfort); rolfing (manipulation of deep body tissue); and therapeutic massage (manipulation of muscle and connective tissue to relieve pain and tension). Holistic health care also commonly includes yoga and meditation techniques discussed in chapter 6.

While most of these holistic techniques involve externally applied therapy, holistic health care also places importance upon diet and internal treatment. Nutritional therapy frequently includes emphasis upon large doses of vitamins, roots, herbs, and other plant derivatives both as treatment for existing conditions and the prevention of potential disorders. Prescription of nutritional therapy often follows unusual (and medically unproven) diagnostic procedures such as hair-shaft analysis and iridology (examination of the iris of the eye).

The advocacy of vegetarianism represents a common nutritional aspect of holistic health frequently practiced by New Agers. Although the overconsumption of red meat in the American diet has been scientifically linked with cardiac and carcinogenic conditions, the total elimination of red meat from the diet is not in keeping with the dietary laws put forth in the Old Testament, particularly in Leviticus 11. Not surprisingly, the Bible, set forth by the omniscient Creator of the human body, provides dietary guidelines for the maintenance of good health and development of disciplined habits of eating.

Almost certainly, connections may be made between the strict vegetarianism of Hinduism and Buddhism and the appeal of such a diet among New Agers. Most recently, some New Agers have taken their dietary restrictions a step beyond vegetarianism and are advocating fruitarianism. The intriguing explanation lies in the interpretation of the Genesis account of the temptation of Adam and Eve. Fruitarians suggest that if Adam and Eve were prohibited from eating the fruit of a certain tree lest they become like God, then fruit must hold a nutritional key to unlocking god-consciousness!

Finally, the realm of holistic health encompasses techniques which, in primitive societies, would most certainly be labeled shamanistic. What is a shaman? In simple terms, he is a medicine man. In more sophisticated Western terms, he is one who deliberately alters his own state of consciousness in order to contact the spirit world for the purpose of gaining power to help (or manipulate) another person. Ironically, shamanistic techniques once confined to primitive cultures are now being described as "scientific" and have been incorporated into the arena of holistic health.

Specifically, persons suffering from a variety of illnesses, ranging from mild to terminal, are encouraged to enter into a meditative state in order to contact an "inner guide" who will then help them "visualize" their bodies as healthy This "guide" is explained as a friendly spirit concerned for the person's welfare and one who will lead the patient to wholeness. A patient may be encouraged to visualize the spirit guide in the act of destroying cancer cells or shrinking a tumor Thus the patient, in effect, becomes his own shaman

Holistic health not only encompasses shamanism but also other occult practices. Hypnosis, psychic healing, folk healing, clairvoyance, and trance-channeling all are employed in various ways to attempt healing of body, mind, and spirit. The dangers of occult involvement have been clearly documented and were discussed at greater length in chapter 7

Given all this information, what may we conclude in considering the subject of holistic health care in relation to the New Age Movement? Must we throw out all aspects of holistic health and label them New Age? The answer is no. The goal of a healthy body, mind, and spirit is not antibiblical. Jesus Christ promised that He came to give us an abundant life. Indeed, 1 Corinthians 6:19 refers to our bodies as temples of the Holy Spirit. In the Old Testament, King Asa was rebuked for putting all his hopes in doctors and not seeking help from the Lord for relief of his foot disease (2 Chronicles 16:12). Certainly modern medical research has borne out the benefits of the kind of rest and dietary rules put forth in the Bible.

The appropriate response to holistic health is one of caution in which the would-be patient takes to heart the Latin dictum *caveat emptor*, "let the buyer beware." Unquestionably, holistic health care is intricately linked with principles and beliefs of the New Age, almost to the point of being virtually inseparable. Much of the healing promised by holistic practitioners rests on the emphasis upon self and the divine energy force within.

Anyone considering various aspects of holistic health must bear in mind their origins in Eastern mysticism as well as the influence of the occult within holistic health. The danger lies not only in outright involvement in the occult but also in the possibility of being gradually drawn into the occult by flirting with its outer edges via holistic health. As a natural outgrowth of curiosity, more than one person has been drawn into occult practices from such seemingly innocent interests as biofeedback or self-hypnosis.

With these cautions in mind, ultimately each person, including the Christian, must make an important individual decision when seeking appropriate health care.

9
Business and Education

In keeping with the New Age Movement as the "Human Potential Movement," it should not come as a surprise to learn that an important part of the New Age is the promulgation of "how-to" and "self-help" seminars. A glance through magazines directed toward the business community reveals the extent to which such seminars have become the current vogue. In addition to the seminars themselves, books, tapes, and a range of videocassettes encourage further home study.

Why Do Businesses Get Involved?

The concept of self-actualization or self-realization not only represents a common desire of modern man but also carries with it the suggestion of fulfillment and happiness. The goal "Be all you can be" not only propels people onto the fast track but also offers the heady promise of power.

The promise of power, whether over circumstances or other people, goes all the way back to the Garden of Eden. In the Big Lie of Genesis 3, the promise of godlike status implied the ultimate in power trips, the power to be like God.

Thus at the basis of the proliferation of self-help and self-actualization seminars we once again find the recurrent theme found in almost all that characterizes the New Age Movement: You can be like God because you already have the divine within you. Or, to put it into Hindu terms, the human "atman," the soul, is already part of "Brahman," the universal absolute. All that needs to be done is to release that "divine within," and any person can achieve maximum potential and reach self-actualization. From its Garden of Eden origins via its path through Hinduism, this deceptive promise has now become big business in the Western world.

In a lengthy article dated May 4, 1987, *Newsweek* aptly used the term *Corporate Mind Control* to describe the many ways in which the business community has bought into the New Age Movement, perhaps to the extent of $4 billion per year. The article cites the names of such foremost American companies as Pacific Bell, Procter & Gamble, TRW, Ford Motor Company, Polaroid, General Mills, and Boeing, all of whom have paid large sums of money for motivational seminars intended to encourage employees to alter their thinking. Of course, the hope these companies harbor is that increased productivity as a result of employee self-realization will bring in more profits, thus making the high cost of such seminars well worth the investment. New Age gurus, willing to turn the cry for spiritualism into dollars, are only too happy to oblige.

The same article mentions Werner Erhard who, in the 1970s, founded a somewhat controversial self-improvement program called "est" aimed at consciousness-raising for individuals. In the 1980s Erhard went corporate, transferring his mind-altering techniques to the business world in the form of Transpersonal Technologies, a company that sells seminars of varying length. In 1986 alone, Transpersonal Technologies' billings totaled $15 million. Erhard's other enterprise, the Forum, now offers a "personal effectiveness course" at a cost of $525, designed to unleash individual creative potential by getting in touch with the "Being." Occasional follow-up workshops (at an additional fee) are available to see to it that clients maintain contact with the "Being."

Not only has Erhard invaded the American corporate structure but he has now gone international as well. According to the *Wall Street Journal* (December 3, 1986), Erhard was given a three-year contract with the Soviet Union to bring the motivational techniques to the Soviet bureaucracy. Perhaps the Soviets did not want to be outdone by the American government, which has also availed itself of Erhard's services. NASA paid Transformational Technologies $45,000 for a five-day seminar to motivate some of its leading engineers. Similarly, SportsMind, Inc., of Seattle earned a $350,000 contract with the U.S. Army to motivate Green Berets. As a result, Green Berets were taught meditation techniques to help them make instant, high-pressure decisions.

Others have learned from Erhard's example and, like the Forum, use a combination of group activities: dancing, singing, confessions, meditations, hugging, and even confrontation. For example, Lifespring, a self-help organization, now totals over two hundred thousand graduates. An organization in Massachusetts called DMA offers techniques designed to encourage employees to visualize a company the way they want it and then to unleash the power of their imaginations to accomplish their goal. Like Lifespring, the titles of motivational companies can be misleading. Innovation Associates of Boston is really a firm dedicated to helping the corporate world become *metanoic*, a Greek term for gaining a clear vision. Those who attend the four-day seminars are taught "holistic systemic thinking."

Another motivational guru whose promises of self-actualization and personal power have become popular is Napoleon Hill, whose work dates back to the 1930s. His principles, neatly packaged in books and tapes, encourage people to "explore the dramatic power of our minds to create self-fulfilling beliefs." Who in a materialistic society could resist Hill's tape series *Think and Grow Rich*? Referred to in catalogs as a classic, this series suggests, "Anything your mind can conceive and believe—you can achieve." One of Hill's books, *The Law of Success*, promises to reveal the "metaphysical secrets" that empowered successful men of history toward positive thinking and subsequent success.

Similarly, the works of best-selling author L. Ron Hubbard promise "health and certainty," "practical exercises to handle exhaustion and stress," as well as personal satisfaction and fulfillment at the workplace. His book *Dianetics: The Evolution of a Science* is advertised as "the Owner's Manual for the Human Mind" and has become hugely successful on the book market. Hubbard's organization, the Church of Scientology, now disperses his lectures around the nation and offers an array of motivational tapes for home and office use.

Closely related to the material of Hill and Hubbard is a whole range of self-improvement books and tapes. In America's major bookstores, entire sections are devoted to the topic. Many books offer stress-management skills, improvement in relationships, and success in "getting what you want." Tapes with such titles as *Slim Forever*, *Stop Smoking Forever*, and *Awaken Your Sensuality* are based on the premise that visualization and subliminal suggestion can break through blocks of negativity and thus release subconscious energy.

Whether in the corporate structure or in the privacy of the home, these human-potential techniques should be carefully examined before being adopted. What places many of them within the context of the New Age Movement is that their origins lie in the belief that there is a divine energy source within each person which, when tapped and released, will give that person the power to create his own reality. Thus reality can be created and also *altered* in order to achieve fulfillment for the individual. Because of the divine within, he can meditate, visualize, imagine, and even *speak* something into existence. This is power. This is success. This is human potential. This is Hinduism in a new guise.

New Age in the Classroom

New Age information and subsequent transformation is not confined exclusively to the business world. The New Age Movement has also made its way into the public-education system of America. Because of the formative influence of both elementary and secondary education in shaping the future of a whole nation, New Age influence in American school systems gives reason for alarm.

Several years ago, educators were encouraged to introduce a new concept into the curriculum known as "Values Clarification" or sometimes referred to as "Basic Principles." These innocuous yet ambiguous terms actually serve as euphemisms for a concept that, taken to its extreme, could produce a generation of amoral young people who do not know the difference between right and wrong. In essence, Values Clarification suggests that each student should have the right to decide for himself what his values shall be without interference or influence from others, particularly parents, clergy, or teachers. At the basis of this principle is the belief that each person is intrinsically good and therefore capable of making good moral choices. Furthermore, such a position presupposes that all values are relative to the individual and not subject to influence by outsiders from the past, present, or future.

Moreover, the use of Values Clarification in the classroom is made easier because of the gradual disappearance of Judeo-Christian principles in today's textbooks. For example, a review of one of the leading World History textbooks used at the high school level in America reveals that the history of the Jewish nation has been de-emphasized in favor of that of the Greeks and Romans. The very centerpiece of history, the life of Jesus Christ, is only briefly mentioned. The Protestant Reformation has been slighted, as have the Pilgrims. American History is presented nearly devoid of its formative Christian influences. Thus a message is conveyed to the student by not only what is in the textbooks but also by what is not included. Omission becomes as important as inclusion.

Another area of public education with evidence of New Age influence lies in the area of "behavioral modification" through such techniques as meditation, yoga, and deep relaxation methods. Sometimes called "confluent education" or "transformational curriculum," the goal is to encourage students to activate their own energy force, often by getting in touch with an "inner guide." Children are taught to "center" (a commonly used term for meditation), to chant, to visualize, and to create their own reality.

Yoga exercises, deep breathing, and group dynamics such as "love circles" have now become part of the curriculum of many schools. For the gifted and talented, some schools go a step beyond these techniques and actually encourage students to play the "game" Dungeons and Dragons, a sinister, occult-related game now linked to several teenage suicides. This fantasy game involves role-playing and power-controlling schemes in intricate plots and vicious activities, yet it has attained a following across the nation from grade school through the university level.

Finally, America's public school curriculum now includes a very strong emphasis upon "global education." Here again, the term deceives. Few, including Christians, would object to the need to know more about the greater world and its multitude of cultures—a world that was created by a very imaginative God. Moreover, Christians are called to be "world Christians" with hearts of compassion for all of those of every nation and culture whose lives have not yet been touched by Jesus. World Christians are praying, interceding, and evangelizing Christians with a heart for missions.

But the problem with "global education" as it is now being presented in America's schools is that it teaches principles of one world government, of religious syncretism, and of relative morality, all New Age themes. Internationalism and global government are emphasized at the cost of nationalism and patriotism. Cultural relativism is presented with the suggestion that no culture's ethics are right or wrong but that the two are interchangeable: right can become wrong and wrong can become right.

With such relativism, sin becomes an archaic Judeo-Christian teaching that is based upon mythical tradition. Students, so the suggestion goes, must allow their thinking to be "transformed" away from such antiquated teachings as sin and a judgmental God. Parallel to this idea runs the syncretic suggestion that all religions lead in the same direction and will arrive at the same destination. Therefore, students need not think of one religion as preferable to another.

A sampling of the kinds of materials now being marketed either for education at home or in the school may be seen in a Spring 1989 catalog circulated from Potentials Unlimited of Grand Rapids, Michigan. While the Education Series offers audiotapes for improvement of such skills as creative writing and taking exams, subtly inserted are tapes entitled *Hypnosis for Hypnotists* and *Self-Hypnosis*. The same innocuous-looking catalog offers a Metaphysical Series featuring tapes on such occult topics as astral projection and past-life regression. The theme running through the entire catalog, only one of many such marketings, is that of self-help through one's own resources or through tapping into an extraterrestrial spiritual energy source.

A look at other curriculum sources reveals increased

emphasis upon "death education," which has actually served to contribute to the fascination with death, increased suicide rate, and belief in reincarnation now exhibited by many teenagers. Other curriculum materials are designed to promote "conflict resolution," an activity Christian parents need to examine more closely. Conflict resolution often places students who hold certain moral absolutes in situations where they are encouraged to compromise their beliefs.

Thus we see in these trends in public education several concepts which we also find in the New Age Movement. Values clarification and conflict resolution suggest that personal moral choices are relative, a New Age theme discussed earlier in this book. Second, education is gradually becoming increasingly anti-Christian in its bias, also a New Age tenet. Furthermore, techniques such as "centering," yoga, and meditation as well as discussions of the "energy flow" are also part of New Age thinking. Finally, the concepts of syncretism and the plans for one world government, one religion, and one leader can also be found in the increased emphasis upon "global education."

Closely related to the concept of global education and often linked with global issues is that of environmentalism. Few Christians could disagree with the need to protect this fragile planet, delicately created by God and given to us as our temporal home. In Genesis, man was charged with the stewardship of the earth while in Leviticus the nation of Israel was given guidelines for land use. In the Psalms we read, "The earth is the Lord's, and everything in it, the world, and all who live in it" (Psalm 24:1). Yet we are reminded almost daily of man's careless or abusive use of our environment, whether in the form of thrown-away objects, disappearing species, or polluted air and water. Certainly Christians ought to be in the vanguard of those who treat the earth as a gift from God.

Why then might we question environmental education? Certainly not every environmentalist is a New Ager. However, strong New Age influence can be found in certain sectors of the environmental movement. For example, one trend among those who refer to themselves as "deep ecologists" espouses that the earth is self-regulating, living, and evolving. Furthermore, this school of ecology suggests that the earth is female, sometimes referred to as "Gaia" after the Greek goddess of the earth. Deep ecologists advocate getting "in touch" with Gaia's spirit and "listening to her voice." The Apostle Paul warned against just such activity: "They exchanged the truth of God for a lie, and worshiped and served created things rather than the Creator—who is forever praised. Amen" (Romans 1:25).

Pantheism, discussed earlier, infuses spiritual qualities to environmental objects such as trees, rivers, rocks, canyons, etc. Again we see the merging of the Creator and the created, in this case the environment. However, the biblical perspective suggests that nature and the environment are only reflections of who God is and of His infinitely imaginative mind. We could become avid environmentalists who elevate nature to the point of idolatry but still miss the wonder of a relationship with the living Creator through His Son, Jesus.

May we conclude from these trends that America's educational system has been completely taken over by New Agers? Definitely not. But there is enough New Age influence in the educational system to make a perceptible difference and thus cause alarm among parents. What can be done about it? In a pluralistic society where education is largely secular and supported by tax dollars, changing the system on grounds of religious or even moral objections is not an easy task.

One alternative an increasing number of parents have taken is to place their children in private Christian schools or even in home schools. But most parents, either for financial considerations or reasons of accessibility, do not have that option and therefore must work within the system to try to bring about change.

Certainly at the local levels, pressure can be brought to bear on school boards and in school board elections. Parents can also have a role in textbook adoption and curriculum content. Christian teachers should fully research the sources and philosophy behind materials they are asked to use. But above all, parents can most affect their children's education by instilling within them, from early childhood, sound, unwavering biblical principles backed by the living example of the parents themselves In Proverbs 22:6 we are exhorted, "Train a child in the way he should go, and when he is old he will not turn from it."

10
Entertainment

Just as we can see New Age influence in business and education, so we also find it in the entertainment industry.

Movies

A look at New Age influence upon the entertainment sector would be incomplete without a consideration of the role Shirley MacLaine has played in promoting New Age activities. MacLaine, a gifted actress, dancer, and writer, began a mid-life search for deeper meaning and for answers to some of life's dilemmas. Thus her story is not atypical but actually represents a similar spiritual journey taken by many who are now involved in the New Age. However, her fame makes Shirley MacLaine unique.

The spiritual odyssey of Shirley MacLaine gradually took her from Edgar Cayce's books to a trance medium in Sweden and ultimately to a channeler in the Andes mountains of South America. So totally converted was MacLaine that today she has become a spokesperson for the gospel of the New Age. Her books, including *Out on a Limb*, *It's*

All in the Playing, and *Dancing in the Light*, have become best-sellers and have boosted her career. In 1987, *Out on a Limb*, which chronicles MacLaine's spiritual search, was made into a five-hour TV miniseries.

On occasion, MacLaine holds seminars across the nation, charging three hundred dollars per person ("one hundred dollars for mind, one hundred dollars for body, one hundred dollars for spirit," she unabashedly explains). Recently, she purchased a three-hundred-acre tract of land in the mountains of Colorado to house the proposed Uriel Village, a center for meditation, seminars, and special agricultural projects.

The centerpiece of MacLaine's message is that each person is God. "If you do not see me as God, it's because you don't see yourself as God," she told *Time* magazine (December 7, 1987). MacLaine further suggests that good and evil are nonexistent and therefore should not be used to define human behavior. The doctrine of reincarnation, she teaches, was actually included in the Bible but was struck out by a church council of the sixth century. "I'm not the leader of this movement. I'm not a high priestess of New Age concepts. I'm just a human being trying to find some answers about what we're doing here, where we came from and where we're going," MacLaine was quoted in the same *Time* article. A spiritual seeker? Perhaps. But significantly, because of her celebrity status, Shirley MacLaine is taking many along with her on her personal quest.

By no means is Shirley MacLaine the only New Ager in the movie industry. Certainly New Age and occult influence can be found in many Hollywood offerings. A few years ago, moviegoers were frightened for weeks by such movies as *The Omen*, a film about the antichrist, or *The Exorcist*, dealing with demon possession.

While these films were forthright in their dealing with the occult, more recent popular movies contain thinly veiled New Age themes. An excellent example is Steven Spielberg's phenomenally successful *E.T.*, which grossed over $619 million and has now been released to the huge home videotape audience. In this seemingly innocent movie, a grotesque creature of extraterrestrial origin appears lovable and a friend of children. He communicates through mental telepathy and has spiritual powers to heal and levitate. A whole generation of young moviegoers was thus conditioned to welcome such a creature and to consider such an appearance normal.

Another Spielberg movie, also a huge box office success, is *Close Encounters of the Third Kind*. Like much of the New Age (and like *E.T.*), *Close Encounters* is immensely subtle in its underlying message. Again we have the theme of an extraterrestrial visitation. Here, however, the humans who make contact with the extraterrestrial are drawn by an unnamed and irresistible impulse which they cannot explain. It is apparent that such contact with these unusual beings occurs only with certain selected humans who are in a state of readiness and spiritual awareness. Such extraterrestrial contact is made to appear desirable and even a state to be sought after.

But in promoting a New Age message, perhaps the most powerful movies were the *Star Wars* trilogy of George Lucas. Hugely successful at the box office, these films also dealt with contact between humans and extraterrestrial beings, depicted in varying forms from the lovable to the grotesque. Because the sound effects, cinematography, and film technology were astounding, the *Star Wars* movies had a profound effect upon the audience. But what lingered on in moviegoers' minds was the often-repeated statement, "May the Force be with you."

In keeping with the New Age, *Star Wars* eliminated the Judeo-Christian concept of an infinite and personal God and replaced Him with the Force. The Force represents a great universal energy force within every person. The Force may also be compared with Brahman, the Absolute, of Hinduism, with whom all souls will eventually merge. As a result of *Star Wars*, a whole generation of young people has been conditioned to accept the concept of a universal energy force rather than a personal God to whom they are accountable but with whom they can have a personal and loving relationship.

Television

In addition to the large screen, the small screen in America's living rooms has also become the purveyor of New Age influence. The average child spends forty-four days a year in front of the TV, which has now become one of the major determinants of his value system. TV cartoons, the Saturday-morning fare for millions of American children, feature a subtle array of creatures, power figures, the extraterrestrial, and even the occult. Donald Duck and Woody Woodpecker have gradually given way to the likes of "She-Ra," "Thundercats," and "Bravestar."

She-Ra, fashioned after the Egyptian sun goddess as well as the ancient mystery harlot of Babylon, rides about on a unicorn with rainbow-colored wings, moving between one world and another, flashing her supernatural powers. "She-Ra" has gone beyond simple Cinderella-type fantasy into the realm of the supernatural and occult. Likewise, "Thundercats" features supernatural powers, spirit contact, and sorcery. Similarly, in "Bravestar" children see a shaman who trains the hero to call upon demonic powers to accomplish his mighty deeds.

Video Games

A consideration of both New Age and occult influence in children's entertainment would be incomplete without a look at the craze of the early 1990s: Nintendo. To their great delight, millions of children have discovered Nintendo under their Christmas trees. In order to play the increasing variety of video games offered by the Japanese-based Nintendo company, one must purchase the basic $99.99 grouping, which includes the control box, gun, and control pads. Thereafter, a host of video games ranging from "Mario Brothers" to football and tennis games are available. Many are innocuous. Unfortunately, some are not. Among the more popular choices are "Dragon Warrior," in which the player works his way through an endless variety of mazes at various levels, a process that may take up to a month to play.

Another Nintendo offering, "Shadowgate," is closely related to "Dungeons and Dragons" in its principles of the creation of a sinister kingdom of power and evil. "Shadowgate" may take as long as two or three months to play and particularly appeals to teenagers as well as adults.

Unquestionably, however, the most popular Nintendo offering is the video version of what has become a multimillion-dollar industry: "Teenage Mutant Ninja Turtles." Despite their relatively quiet start as comic book characters in 1983, suddenly the Turtles are everywhere: in a TV cartoon seen on some 130 television stations, as toys, on T-shirts, as children's breakfast cereal, and ultimately in a blockbuster movie which grossed $50 million its first two weeks in the theaters. Adults may chuckle at the slightly sinister looking, wisecracking turtles with such Renaissance names as Donatello, Michelangelo, Raphael, and Leonardo. Granted, these are not Mickey Mouse, Donald Duck, and Goofy, but many might ask, "What is the danger?"

Perhaps a look at what is behind the "Teenage Mutant Ninja Turtles" might help parents make a decision regarding the Ninja Turtle phenomenon. The story line suggests that four turtles were accidentally dropped into the sewer system of Manhattan, whereupon they were exposed to radiation and mutated into teenage turtles. Taken in by a wise old rat who had been trained by a Zen master, the turtles were taught to fight like Ninja warriors.

Aside from the thinly veiled Zen message, the Ninja escapades feature violence and power struggles. Because the chief constituency of the Ninja Turtle craze seems to be small children, parents might well be concerned by the dark undertones purveyed in a world in which one usually expects small children to delight in an array of brightness and color. Are young children able to separate reality from fantasy when the fantasy is represented in such combative form?

Moreover, the common theme not just of the Ninja Turtle exploits but also of many of the video games seen both at home and in arcades is that of power and of the creation of one's own reality. The game player, often using a "gun," becomes a power broker, the controlling master who dominates a world he can create as well as alter. Individual power is the projection of the self by means of control and manipulation. What will be the influence on society of a whole generation of young people who emerge into adulthood having feasted on a diet of power games and combative ventures?

Finally, the very nature of video games and the way in which they are used may well be subject to question, particularly by Christian parents. Whether played at home or in the thousands of darkened and noisy arcades which dot the cities of Europe and America, video games possess a singularly unique ability to become obsessively addictive. Children, adolescents, and even adults may find themselves seduced into spending endless hours before the video screen at the expense of more physically and spiritually healthy activities.

Music

For an older audience, the New Age now comprises a significant sector of the music industry. Even the Grammys list a separate award category called New Age Music. In many parts of the country, New Age music is now among the highest-selling categories of music. Some radio stations, particularly FM stations, now exclusively feature New Age music, while others feature weekly programs of New Age music such as "Hearts of Space," now heard on over two hundred stations. Most recently, some record stores have broadened the New Age musical category by simply labeling it "Adult Contemporary," a much more pleasing and acceptable term.

But what is New Age music? How can New Age thinking be transferred to music? Those who are devoted to it say New Age music cannot be put into words. While occasionally dissonant in sound, the music is usually meditative and designed to put the listener in "another state." Some devotees say it puts them in a "different place." Instrumentation varies from piano, harp, guitar, and synthesizer to Tibetan temple bells, Japanese shamisen, Indian sitar, or even such a bizarre instrument as a sheet of steel balanced on a balloon of water. Repetitious themes and experimentation seemingly without pattern also characterize this new and important movement in music.

Some call the music "mellow," while others refer to it as "spiritual," and still others call it "Yuppie Muzak" or "Pablum for Baby Boomers." Often FM stations deliberately schedule the music during rush-hour traffic periods for weary office workers on their way home. Among the musical artists whose work is called New Age are Andres Vollenweider, George Zamfir, and Stephen Halpern. But perhaps the best known is Kitaro, the Japanese composer-musician. During an American tour, Kitaro referred to New Age music as music to "make oneself aware of the moment."

Whatever the attempt to describe New Age music, one significant fact remains: The music is often deliberately used to move the listener into a meditative state and is frequently used as an accompaniment to Eastern mystical practices. The artistic representations on record jackets often feature landscapes or ethereal, misty scenes. Titles of albums and of separate compositions also give some indication of content. Among the long list of examples, *Om Namah Shuvaya*, by Robbie Gass, is ninety minutes of Sanskrit chants set to guitars and organ. *One Light* by Michael Stillwater focuses on "spiritual transformation." Stephen Halpern's *Mellow Moments* is openly advertised as a "New Age repertoire and guaranteed relaxation music." Maloah Stillwater's *Shores of Paradise* features ocean and tropical sounds in the background and is suggested as ideal for massage or for putting children to sleep.

Because Christianity also offers its own versions of quiet, meditative music, one must examine both the belief system of the artist as well as the intent of the music. Is the artist a committed Christian whose faith is biblically based? Is the music designed to turn the listener toward worship of the most high God? Just as the difference between Christian meditation and Eastern meditation is that the former turns one *upward* toward an infinite, personal God while the latter turns one *inward* toward the "god within," so a distinctive difference lies between Christian meditative music and New Age music.

As we have seen, the New Age Movement offers something for everyone, from holistic health to meditative music. Now that we know the facts, let us consider our reaction to what is happening around us.

V

HOW DO WE RESPOND?

11
A Changing Worldview

Is the New Age Movement a passing phase destined for history's trash bin along with the Charleston of the twenties and three-dimensional movies of the fifties? Or, does the New Age Movement represent a significant trend in Western culture about which Christians need to be both informed and concerned?

When we consider the numbers of people involved in one way or another in some aspect of the New Age Movement, coupled with the influence New Age thinking has in such areas as entertainment, health care, business, and education, one can conclude that the New Age Movement is more than just a passing fad. Moreover, from a biblical perspective, the New Age may be viewed as a significant fulfillment of those biblical definitions and warnings concerning the spirit of the antichrist, although one is well advised to exercise caution in suggesting with finality that the New Age Movement will actually produce the antichrist himself.

While such practices as transcendental meditation, yoga, channeling, crystal consciousness, as well as the belief in reincarnation and astrology violate biblical principles, these activities represent aspects of something much larger that is taking place in Western culture. What we are seeing in the United States, Western Europe, and Australia is a significant shift away from a Western worldview based upon certain Judeo-Christian traditions to an Eastern worldview based upon Hindu, Buddhist, and Taoist influences. This fact alone should trigger alarm among Christians. Possibly as much as 20 percent of the American populace has shifted from a Western to an Eastern worldview, or a hybrid of the two, in recent years.

What Is the Western Worldview?

The Western worldview, based upon certain Judeo-Christian traditions, was transmitted into Western thinking through influential institutions, including the Church, government, and educational institutions, particularly as a result of the Reformation. Perhaps the most significant aspect of the Judeo-Christian tradition is the concept that God is an infinite Being who is both sovereign and personal. Not only is He infinite and personal but particular characteristics set Him apart from mankind as well: He is omniscient, omnipotent, and omnipresent. This concept of God not only influenced European institutions but also undergirded the very foundation of the Thirteen Colonies and made its way into the establishment of the United States of America more than two centuries ago.

A second notable characteristic of the Western worldview as influenced by Judeo-Christian tradition lies in its linear interpretation of history. History is viewed as a straight line beginning at a particular point in time and space and proceeding toward a specific preordained end. Furthermore, this grand sweep of history is filled with historical events controlled by the sovereignty of an omniscient God. Thus, history not only contains meaning but also moves in a specific direction; world events are not out of control; divine purposes are being accomplished; God's sovereignty is made manifest.

Third, the traditional Western worldview based upon Judeo-Christian principles suggests the existence of certain moral and ethical absolutes which, when adhered to, stabilize the underpinnings of a society. Foremost among these absolutes are the definitions of right and wrong, good and evil, truth and falsehood. The absolute standards of right, of good, and of truth are based upon an absolute and unchanging God who said of Himself, "I the Lord do not change" (Malachi 3:6). Thus He becomes the essence of all that is good, all that is truth, and all that is right. Upon such unchangeable standards the laws of man can be based, measurements of justice meted, and society may function in an orderly and peaceful manner.

Also included in this Judeo-Christian concept of absolute ethical and moral standards is the belief in sin. *Sin* may be defined as those actions and thoughts which separate one from a perfect and holy God. In his introduction to John Owen's classic *Sin & Temptation*, theologian J. I. Packer writes, "Sin disorders the soul and disintegrates the character."[1] The acknowledgment of sin runs through both the Old Testament and New Testament and provides the reason for God's greatest gift of love, Jesus Christ, who became a ransom for sin.

Finally, in the traditional Judeo-Christian worldview, man is recognized as a divinely created being and thus unique. Created in God's own image, man is described by the Psalmist as "a little lower than the heavenly beings and crowned . . . with glory and honor" (Psalm 8:5). This "divine stamp" forever provides man with a point of identification that separates him from all other creation. Man's uniqueness and inestimable value to God is attested by the heavenly Father's fathomless gift of His Son, Jesus, as a sacrifice to redeem mankind.

Thus, the concept of God; the perception of history, its movement and meaning; the belief in moral absolutes, including an acknowledgment of sin; and the view of man as a unique being have each played a major role in forming the Western worldview and in establishing major Western institutions. Significantly, this worldview is now gradually shifting to what may be termed an Eastern worldview, which finds its origins in the religions of Asia and the ancient Near East.

What Is the Eastern Worldview?

We may better gain an understanding of an Eastern worldview by contrasting its major principles to those of the West. In contrast to the Western concept of a singular God who is infinite and personal, the Eastern worldview suggests that God is a transcendent energy force, a pervasive universal spirit whose existence is actually multiplied and manifested in infinite numbers in the form of human beings. Thus every human being is God and capable of maintaining sovereignty over his own life. Unlike the Judeo-Christian separation of God from man, this

Hindu-Buddhist concept merges the Creator and created into one.

Second, whereas the Western worldview interprets history from a linear perspective in which events have meaning and purpose under the control of a sovereign God, the Eastern worldview suggests that history consists of cosmic cycles, each of which is something of a closed circle. Within a cosmic cycle, all beings work their way through a repeated pattern of births and rebirths (reincarnation) until at last they reach a point of release into transcendent oneness with the Absolute Energy Force. Events within the cosmic cycle are controlled not by an omniscient God but by the uncertainties of karma, the law of cause and effect. Thus the entire understanding of space and time is different within the closed system represented by the Eastern worldview in contrast to that of the West.

Likewise, the concept of moral and ethical absolutes is different within these two worldviews. Because of the influence of karma and reincarnation, absolute standards such as truth and goodness give way to relative standards. If all is changing and in a state of cosmic flux, no absolutes exist. Even the Hindu concept of the Absolute, Brahman, is that he can be both good and evil as well as right and wrong. Similarly, the ancient Chinese philosophy of Taoism, which has had such a profound influence upon East Asia, suggests that all things are constantly changing. Good can become evil, right can become wrong, light can become darkness, etc. The concept of sin is nonexistent in such thinking. Thus all of life and everything connected with it becomes relative.

Not surprisingly, such a worldview places man within a different context as well. Whereas the Judeo-Christian worldview elevates man because of his divinely created existence, a Hindu-Buddhist worldview places man within the cosmic cycle of reincarnation, governed by the Law of karma, and thus reduces the uniqueness and individuality of each person. Disease, sickness, poverty, and calamity are greeted with less compassion because such occurrences are simply attributed to karma.

If in fact a significant number of Westerners, particularly those involved in some aspect of the New Age Movement, allow their worldview and personal belief systems to slip into a Hindu-Buddhist framework, the potential exists for a serious, even if gradual, erosion of Judeo-Christian values in major Western institutions and should arouse great concern, particularly among Christians.

12
The Christian Response

If the New Age Movement represents Asian religions brought to America's doorstep, what response is needed on the part of Christians? Three responses are possible. First, some will opt for the "ostrich" approach in which Christians either ignore the existence of the New Age Movement or dismiss it as another fad which will soon pass. Even more serious would be a casual attitude which responds with aloofness, "Oh, well. To each his own," and thus avoids any confrontation.

A second response may be the opposite extreme of seeing New Age influence everyplace and in everything. Such an overreaction may stimulate undue suspicion, which in turn breeds fear and misunderstanding. There is not a New Ager hiding behind every bush. While many, many people have naively inculcated some aspect of New Age thinking into their personal philosophy or some New Age activity into their life-style, this does not necessarily define them as New Agers. However, as explained earlier in this book, the nature of New Age activity is that many people are easily drawn from peripheral involvement into much deeper New Age entanglement. Therein lies a very important reason for caution and understanding.

The third and most appropriate response on the part of Christians is to recognize the activity of the New Age Movement as a significant trend in both the United States and Western Europe that is gradually changing the way millions of people think and thus exerts an influence on business, education, entertainment, and health care. If taken to its extreme and given the accomplishment of the goals of its leadership, the New Age Movement would inaugurate one world government and one world religion under one ruler.

When we turn to the Bible for understanding of what is happening, we find that characteristics of the New Age Movement bear out warnings and partial fulfillment of prophecies. Jesus foretold in Matthew 24:4, 5: "Watch out that no one deceives you. For many will come in my name, claiming, 'I am the Christ,' and will deceive many." Later, in the same discourse, Jesus warns, "At that time many will turn away from the faith and will betray and hate each other, and many false prophets will appear and deceive many people" (verses 10, 11). This was His response to the disciples' question concerning the signs of His coming and of the end of the age.

As we look at the characteristics of the New Age Movement, the Apostle Paul's warning to the Church at Thessalonica also becomes very relevant:

The coming of the lawless one will be in accordance with the work of Satan displayed in all kinds of counterfeit miracles, signs and wonders, and in every sort of evil that deceives those who are perishing. They perish because they refused to love the truth and so be saved. For this reason God sends them a powerful delusion so that they will believe the lie.

2 Thessalonians 2:9–11

By virtue of its denial of the Lordship of Jesus Christ and its perpetuation of the lie that every person is his own god, the New Age Movement fails the biblical litmus test of truth and falls within the category of the spirit of the antichrist as defined in 1 John 4:1–3:

Dear friends, do not believe every spirit, but test the spirits to see whether they are from God, because many false prophets have gone out into the world. This is how you can recognize the Spirit of God: Every spirit that acknowledges that Jesus Christ has come in the flesh is from God, but every spirit that does not acknowledge Jesus is not from God. This is the spirit of the antichrist, which you have heard is coming and even now is already in the world.

Answering New Agers

An important aspect of the subtlety of the New Age Movement may be found in its appealing yet misleading vocabulary, which at times sounds both Christian and biblical. Thus a conversation with a New Ager may become the setting for miscommunication and misunderstanding unless terms are carefully defined. This fact demands that Christians not only practice discernment but also possess a knowledge of the Scriptures as well as a firm grasp of their own beliefs. New Age terminology represents an excellent example of the way darkness masquerades as light and thus deceives many.

Perhaps the most deceptive use of a Christian term by New Agers is found in references to "Christ." To a Christian who knows Jesus Christ as Savior and Lord, the name *Christ* can only mean the Jesus Christ of the Bible, the Son of God, who came to earth in the form of a Person who lived in Palestine, was crucified as an atonement for the sins of mankind, and was resurrected into glory. But to New Agers the name *Christ* represents a spiritually enlightened figure who can exist in any culture at any time. Thus Jesus of Nazareth was one of a list that also includes Krishna, Gautama Buddha, Muhammad, Lao-tzu, and numerous others. Furthermore, according to New Agers, every person has the potential of reaching such a point of spiritual enlightenment if he realizes his "Christ-consciousness." Thus Christians and New Agers are poles apart in their understanding of the name *Christ*.

Similarly, New Agers make references to being "god-like." This means one should tap into the divine energy force within and recognize that each person is actually God. The Bible, on the other hand, exhorts us to live godly lives:

> For the grace of God that brings salvation has appeared to all men. It teaches us to say "No" to

ungodliness and worldly passions, and to live self-controlled, upright and godly lives in this present age, while we wait for the blessed hope—the glorious appearing of our great God and Savior, Jesus Christ.

Titus 2:11–13

The Christian goal of godliness will never make one godlike because God, the Creator, will always remain separate from man, the created. This arrangement is to man's benefit because it allows him to have a wonderfully fulfilling and intimate relationship with the living God, a relationship that could not thrive if man were himself God.

Another favorite buzzword of the New Age Movement is *transformation*. The "new age" itself will represent a transformation of all mankind into the Age of Aquarius, an era of peace and harmony. This state of being will be accomplished on a personal level when individuals are transformed by a moment of spiritual enlightenment. Here again, the term is deceptive. The Bible exhorts us to be "transformed by the renewing of your mind" (Romans 12:2). For the Christian, this transformation is best explained as putting on the "new self" (Ephesians 4:24) or, as Paul explains, "Therefore, if anyone is in Christ, he is a new creation; the old has gone, the new has come!" (2 Corinthians 5:17). This transformation in the life of a Christian is a gradual process aided by the presence of the Holy Spirit and not a flash of personal insight, as New Agers perceive it.

Closely related to transformation are the New Age concepts of meditation and enlightenment. As explained in an earlier chapter, Christian meditation and New Age meditation such as transcendental or Zen meditation are quite different from each other. Whereas New Age forms of meditation, primarily borrowed from Hinduism and Buddhism, cause the meditator to turn his thoughts inward, Christian meditation turns thoughts upward toward God in thankfulness, adoration, and worship.

Likewise, New Agers use the term *enlightenment* differently from Christians. For the New Ager, enlightenment represents a flash of spiritual insight which often occurs during an altered state of consciousness such as meditation, an occult experience, or while under the influence of a hallucinogenic drug. However, for the Christian, enlightenment comes not from some internally generated flash but from Jesus, who is the Light of the world and from whom comes all spiritual illumination. Jesus, not the Christian himself, remains the Source of light. Describing Jesus, John writes, "In him was life, and that life was the light of men" (John 1:4).

The commonly used New Age term *self-fulfillment* is also variously referred to as "self-actualization" or achievement of "human potential." Within the New Age context, self-fulfillment comes from activating the divine within and realizing one's godlike status. This comes from "transformational thinking," which then leads to development of full human potential, a process generated from within each person.

Certainly the Bible encourages the exercise of positive faith, particularly in Hebrews 11, the great faith chapter. Similarly, Jesus promises an abundant life: "I have come that they may have life, and have it to the full" (John 10:10). Contrary to the world's system, including New

Age thinking, Christian self-fulfillment comes not from self-actualization but from self-acceptance, the challenge of accepting God's love for us, which then allows us to accept ourselves as He has made us and to yield to His purposes in our lives. We are exhorted to die to those aspects of ourselves that are antagonistic to God's purposes in our lives.

Jesus, who set an example of servanthood, humility, and giving of Himself to others, said, "If anyone would come after me, he must deny himself and take up his cross daily and follow me" (Luke 9:23). Paul, who before his conversion possessed power, status, and scholarly achievement, would later write, "I consider everything a loss compared to the surpassing greatness of knowing Christ Jesus my Lord, for whose sake I have lost all things. I consider them rubbish, that I may gain Christ" (Philippians 3:8). Paul found the secret of self-acceptance by dying to his selfish desires and merging his life into that of Christ, thus allowing the purposes of God to be carried out in his life.

Another New Age term which sounds somehow Christian but which has quite a different meaning is *rebirth*. To a New Ager, the concept of rebirth may have two meanings. It may be a reference to the process of reincarnation, in which a soul is born into human form again and again, or it may be a reference to the personal and planetary transformation for which New Agers are searching.

To a Christian, however, rebirth is a reference to Christ's response to the inquisitive Nicodemus. Jesus says, "I tell you the truth, no one can see the kingdom of God unless he is born again" (John 3:3). Jesus explains that this is not a physical birth but a spiritual birth of water and the Holy Spirit, which thus becomes the entry point into the kingdom of God. For the Christian, to be born again is to acknowledge one's need for Jesus Christ as Savior, to invite Him to become Lord of one's life, and to allow the Holy Spirit to fill one's being.

Finally, a New Age term which sounds Christian but which is very deceptive is *spirit guide*. Many New Agers, particularly those who channel, refer to their spirit guides or supernatural beings whose voices speak to or through humans. Because channeling is forbidden in the Bible, these spirit guides cannot be thought of as angels. Rather, they are demonic beings who come from that third of the angels who were expelled from heaven with Lucifer.

For the Christian, the Holy Spirit, the Third Person of the Trinity, serves as a spiritual guide and counsel. Jesus said of the Holy Spirit, "But when he, the Spirit of truth, comes, he will guide you into all truth" (John 16:13). Jesus also talked of the Holy Spirit's role as a Counselor when He said, "But the Counselor, the Holy Spirit, whom the Father will send in my name, will teach you all things and will remind you of everything I have said to you" (John 14:26).

Thus, the New Age Movement represents a distortion and perversion of all that represents the very heart of Christianity and of that which a generous heavenly Father has provided for His children. The faith in a single infinite personal God is exchanged for belief in a cosmic energy force. The God above is substituted by the god within. Jesus Christ of Nazareth, Savior of the world, becomes one of many Christs. The Holy Spirit is exchanged for a spirit guide. Resurrection is replaced by reincarnation. Meditation on God is altered to meditation within. Finding oneself in Christ is substituted by self-actualization. The list could go on but, in short, the New Age Movement comprises an array of spiritual counterfeits.

13
A Challenge to Christians

The New Age Movement represents both a challenge and an opportunity for Christians. The single most powerful and effective response of Christians to the New Age Movement is a strong, personal, unwavering commitment to Jesus Christ, characterized by a changed life-style that is obedient to God. This comes first from an acknowledgment of personal sin and the need for reconciliation with a holy and perfect God, as explained in Romans 3:23: "For all have sinned and fall short of the glory of God." Paul goes on to explain the results of sin, "For the wages of sin is death . . ." (6:23), but concludes that verse by giving a wonderful promise: ". . . but the gift of God is eternal life in Christ Jesus our Lord." The entire message of the Bible lies in these two verses—a message that a searching world, including New Agers, needs to hear.

Being a Christian means allowing Jesus Christ to be the Lord of one's life, a commitment which requires a concerted act of daily submission. Again, we read the words of Paul: "So then, just as you received Christ Jesus as Lord, continue to live in him" (Colossians 2:6). In 1 Peter 3:15 we read, "But in your hearts set apart Christ as Lord." The day will come when "at the name of Jesus every knee should bow . . . and every tongue confess that Jesus Christ is Lord" (Philippians 2:10, 11).

However, the strongly committed Christian life calls for a courageous life-style, particularly in the face of increasing opposition. Just as soldiers in a temporal war must defend themselves, so Christians are involved in spiritual warfare and an effective Christian understands the nature of spiritual warfare. As in temporal warfare, we need to know who the enemy is. For the Christian, the enemy is not the New Ager but Satan, the fallen Lucifer, a proud and rebellious angel whose expulsion from heaven occurred in the eons of time past and is described in Isaiah 14:12: "How you have fallen from heaven, O morning star, son of the dawn! You have been cast down to the earth. . . ." Jesus Himself, who was with the Father from the beginning, saw Lucifer's expulsion. He told His disciples, "I saw Satan fall like lightning from heaven" (Luke 10:18).

Not only was Satan expelled from heaven but he was accompanied by one third of the angels, as cited in Revelation 12:4: "His tail swept a third of the stars [angels] out of the sky and flung them to the earth." Consequently, the fallen Lucifer and his angels became the Prince of Darkness and ruling principalities and powers of darkness against which Paul warns in Ephesians 6:12: "For our struggle is not against flesh and blood, but against the rulers, against the authorities, against the powers of this dark world and against the spiritual forces of evil in the heavenly realms."

Although Satan controls the earthly, temporal systems as described in 1 John 5:19—"the whole world is under the control of the evil one"—the good news is that in the titanic struggle in the universe between the Kingdom of Light and the powers of darkness, Jesus Christ is Victor. He triumphed over Satan at the cross. Colossians 2:15 tells us what Christ did to the powers of darkness: "he made a public spectacle of them, triumphing over them by the cross."

In the face of mounting opposition, including the distinctive anti-Christian bias of the New Age, Christians need not despair. Anyone who has read the complete Bible knows that in the Book of Revelation, Jesus Christ, the King of Kings and Lord of Lords, will establish His kingdom forever. While at times it may seem that the powers of darkness are advancing in our society and that Christians may be growing battle weary, we must also remember that the kingdom of Jesus Christ is rapidly advancing throughout the world as people from every nation respond to Him. We are assured in 1 John 4:4 that "the one who is in you is greater than the one who is in the world." God is still sovereign and remains very much in control of the destiny of the universe and everything in it.

Because we read in Matthew 24:24, "For false Christs and false prophets will appear and perform great signs and miracles to deceive even the elect—if that were possible," Christians must become so intimately acquainted with the real Jesus Christ of the Bible that they can easily recognize the counterfeit. That familiarity with Jesus is established through prayer, Bible study, and time spent alone with Him—a relationship that necessitates both time and commitment. The urgency of cultivating such a relationship is caused by tumultuous global events which point to the fulfillment of many biblical prophecies describing the last days.

The committed Christian who has found peace and fulfillment in a living relationship with Jesus Christ can offer a great deal to the New Ager. Most persons involved in various aspects of the New Age Movement are spiritual seekers. Many New Agers are in their thirties, forties, or fifties; are well educated; and have good-paying jobs and positions of influence. Ironically, yesterday's flower children have become today's yuppies—and their spiritual hunger remains unsatisfied. The drive for accumulation of more wealth, status, and power has left them spiritually bankrupt. In their spiritual search, many have turned to the New Age for answers.

Unfortunately, the New Age Movement, with all of its spiritual smorgasbord of offerings, cannot fulfill the innermost longing of the human heart. That longing was put there by a Creator God who is also a loving Father and who longs to have a relationship with His children. When that relationship is established through the person of His Son, Jesus Christ, the human spirit at last comes home and the soul finds rest.

The invitation of Jesus, "Come to me, all you who are weary and burdened, and I will give you rest" (Matthew 11:28), remains a standing invitation as timely today as when it was first issued. In Jesus Christ millions have found peace, love, transformation, and fulfillment—all goals sought by New Agers. The New Age Movement represents an opportunity for Christians to reach out in love and compassion to spiritual seekers in order to offer them the greatest gift of all, the gift of salvation and eternal life through Jesus Christ.

Yes, a new age *is* coming: a glorious age of peace, righteousness, and love. But the coming new age is not the Age of Aquarius. This great day will begin when Jesus, the King of Kings and Lord of Lords, establishes His kingdom forever. He will reign in majesty, glory, and splendor, exercising righteousness, love, and truth. The Book of Daniel, written some twenty-four hundred years ago, describes this glorious event: "He was given authority, glory and sovereign power; all peoples, nations and men of every language worshiped him. His dominion is an everlasting dominion that will not pass away, and his kingdom is one that will never be destroyed" (Daniel 7:14).

There will be a new heaven and a new earth in which "the dwelling of God is with men, and he will live with them. They will be his people, and God himself will be with them and be their God" (Revelation 21:3). Well might we join the beloved apostle in his response: "Amen. Come, Lord Jesus" (Revelation 22:20).

Source Notes

Chapter 2 Defining Our Terms

1. Dr. Karl Menninger, *Whatever Became of Sin?* (New York: Hawthorne Books, 1973).

Chapter 3 Back to the Roots

1. V. S. Naipaul, *India: A Wounded Civilization* (London: Andre Deutsch Ltd., 1977).

Chapter 5 Toward the Age of Aquarius

1. *The Christian Science Monitor*, February 8, 1990, p. 9.
2. *See* Constance Cumbey, *The Hidden Dangers of the Rainbow* (Shreveport, Louisiana: Huntington House, 1983), p. 218.
3. Ibid., p. 200.
4. J. Gordon Melton, et al., *New Age Encyclopedia* (Detroit: Gale Research, Inc., 1990), p. 239.

Chapter 7 Occult New Age

1. *U.S. News & World Report*, February 9, 1987.
2. *West Hawaii Today*, April 24, 1988.
3. *Time*, December 15, 1986, p. 36.
4. *Nexus*, Winter 1988, p. 4.
5. Robert Morey, "When Christians Meet Astrology," *Christianity Today*, December 1988, p. 23.

Chapter 11 A Changing Worldview

1. John Owen, *Sin & Temptation* (Portland, Oregon: Multnomah Press, 1983), p. xx.

Suggestions for Further Reading

Albrecht, Mark C. *Reincarnation: A Christian Critique of a New Age Doctrine*. Downers Grove, Illinois: InterVarsity Press, Inc., 1982.

Anderson, J. N. D. *Christianity & Comparative Religion*. Downers Grove, Illinois: InterVarsity Press, Inc., 1977.

Boa, Kenneth. *Cults, World Religions, and You*. Wheaton, Illinois: Victor Books, 1986.

Carr, Joseph. *The Lucifer Connection*. Lafayette, Louisiana: Huntington House, Inc., 1987.

Chandler, Russell. *Understanding the New Age*. Dallas, Texas: Word Publishers, 1989.

Cumbey, Constance. *The Hidden Dangers of the Rainbow: The New Age Movement and Our Coming Age of Barbarism*. Shreveport, Louisiana: Huntington House, Inc., 1983.

Groothius, Douglas. *Confronting the New Age: How to Resist a Growing Religious Movement*. Downers Grove, Illinois: InterVarsity Press, Inc., 1988.

———. *Unmasking the New Age*. Downers Grove, Illinois: InterVarsity Press, Inc., 1986.

Hunt, Dave. *The Cult Explosion*. Eugene, Oregon: Harvest House Publishers, 1980.

────── and T. R. McMahon. *America, The Sorcerer's New Apprentice: The Rise of New Age Shamanism*. Eugene, Oregon: Harvest House Publishers, 1988.

Lewis, Gordon R. *What Everyone Should Know About Transcendental Meditation*. Glendale, California: Regal Books, 1977.

Marrs, Texe. *Dark Secrets of the New Age*. Westchester, Illinois: Crossway Books, 1987.

Martin, Walter. *The Kingdom of the Cults*. Minneapolis, Minnesota: Bethany House, 1988.

Matrisciana, Caryl. *Gods of the New Age*. Eugene, Oregon: Harvest House, 1985.

Petersen, William J. *Those Curious New Cults in the 80s*. New Canaan, Connecticut: Keats Publishing, Inc., 1982.